Finding a Future That Fits

ACHIEVE YOUR DREAMS & DISCOVER YOUR TRUE SELF

LOUISE PRESLEY-TURNER

HAY HOUSE

Australia • Canada • Hong Kong • India
South Africa • United Kingdom • United States

Published and distributed in the United Kingdom by:
Hay House UK Ltd, 292B Kensal Rd, London W10 5BE.
Tel.: (44) 20 8962 1230; Fax: (44) 20 8962 1239.
www.hayhouse.co.uk

Published and distributed in the United States of America by:
Hay House, Inc., PO Box 5100, Carlsbad, CA 92018-5100.
Tel.: (1) 760 431 7695 or (800) 654 5126;
Fax: (1) 760 431 6948 or (800) 650 5115.
www.hayhouse.com

Published and distributed in Australia by:
Hay House Australia Ltd, 18/36 Ralph St, Alexandria NSW 2015.
Tel.: (61) 2 9669 4299; Fax: (61) 2 9669 4144.
www.hayhouse.com.au

Published and distributed in the Republic of South Africa by:
Hay House SA (Pty), Ltd, PO Box 990, Witkoppen 2068.
Tel./Fax: (27) 11 467 8904.
www.hayhouse.co.za

Published and distributed in India by:
Hay House Publishers India, Muskaan Complex, Plot No.3, B-2,
Vasant Kunj, New Delhi – 110 070. Tel.: (91) 11 4176 1620; Fax: (91) 11 4176 1630.
www.hayhouse.co.in

Distributed in Canada by:
Raincoast, 9050 Shaughnessy St, Vancouver, BC V6P 6E5.
Tel.: (1) 604 323 7100; Fax: (1) 604 323 2600

Text © Louise Presley-Turner, 2009, 2012

The moral rights of the author have been asserted.

The information given in this book should not be treated as a substitute for professional medical advice; always consult a medical practitioner. Any use of information in this book is at the reader's discretion and risk. Neither the author nor the publisher can be held responsible for any loss, claim or damage arising out of the use, or misuse, or the suggestions made or the failure to take medical advice.

A catalogue record for this book is available from the British Library.

This book was previously published by AuthorHouse, ISBN 978-1-4490-1123-9

ISBN: 978-1-84850-810-1

Printed and bound in Great Britain by TJ International, Padstow, Cornwall.

To my beautiful children:

May you achieve every goal and ambition set.
May you live a full and rich life.
May you be blessed with ever-lasting love.
May you appreciate every second of your wonderful life.
But above all, may you always be happy.
I love you.

Contents

Acknowledgements

I'd like to acknowledge all those who have had faith in me while I've been writing this book. I'd also like to acknowledge all the wonderful authors who have inspired and helped me grow over the years. But above all, I want to thank my husband for all his love and support – I simply wouldn't be where I am today without you!

Introduction

I WANT MORE FROM LIFE THAN THIS...

This book is for you if:

- You wake up each morning feeling tired and apathetic.

- You feel let down by life and find yourself saying, 'There must be a better way!'

- You feel time is speeding up and your life is passing you by.

- You're completely bored with your current job.

- Your relationships aren't what they should be.

- You don't like who you have become.

- You know you deserve to live a better life.

- You long for inner fulfilment and happiness.

- You're ready to make some big changes to your life.

- You're open and committed to finding a better way to live.

Congratulations! However you have come to be holding this book, whether it was given to you by a friend, family member or colleague, or maybe you just liked the cover among all the other hundreds of self-help books on the shelf; whatever the reason, I want you to know that you hold in your hands a book that has the potential to change your life in unimaginable ways. Yes, really!

You have officially taken the first step towards creating the life you know you deserve. You've decided that something's not working, and you're ready to make some changes for the better. This is more than most people do in their entire lifetime. This book is designed to get you out of your rut and wake you up to who you really are and what you really want from life. But, before I go on to explain more about its content and how it works, let me share with you my story and the inspiration that led me to write this book.

I REMEMBER THE TURNING-POINT IN MY LIFE LIKE IT WAS ONLY YESTERDAY

Like most of us, I had been busy plodding along, well and truly stuck in a rut, the daily grind of life. Work, sleep, work, sleep... you know the form. Some days were easier than others, but, on the whole, they all seemed to blend into one, and the years whizzed by at such an alarming speed I was left gasping for air.

I wasn't unhappy; far from it. I realized my blessings and was grateful for them, but I wasn't ecstatic about life, either. Something deep inside was missing and I couldn't quite put my finger on it. Externally I had it all: beautiful house in the country, loving and supportive husband, a wonderful daughter, a great lifestyle with lots of holidays. But something was definitely missing. I couldn't put my finger on it. I looked around and it appeared to me that everyone else was in the same rut, doing the same things, so I convinced myself that this was just how life was supposed to be and carried on with the status quo.

There were times when I remember looking at the sky on a beautiful balmy summer evening, when the last of the day's sunshine was breaking through the clouds, casting wonderful, vivid pink and orange rays, and I'd think to myself, 'What is this all about? Why are we here?' In those rare moments, without doubt, I knew that the heavens were calling me to dig a little deeper to find the answer to my own question, and I vowed that one day, when I had more time, money, wisdom and so on, I'd find out. Deep down I knew there was something else I should be doing with my life, but, of course, like so many of us, I ignored the feeling and carried on filling my life with things that I thought were important until I forgot about my deeper quest for meaning and purpose.

Until one day a book called *Excuse Me, Your Life Is Waiting* landed on my doorstep. This book was like no other I'd come across before, and little did I know at the time that it was to change my life. Having read it, I had unknowingly evoked an almighty power, and opened a door into a magical and mystical world of self-discovery, not only for myself but also encompassing questions concerning human existence. The veil was lifted and I was about to reveal the real me!

My journey so far (and I'm still travelling) has been a mixture of highs and lows, but for the first time in my life I have found my calling. I want to help you do the same! By doing so your life will turn a corner, and instead of travelling haphazardly through life, letting the wind take you wherever it will, you can, for the first time, take control and steer yourself towards a happier and more fulfilling future. Does this sound too good to be true? I know it does, but the truth is right in front of your eyes. It's so simple, yet most of us overlook it because we have never stopped for a second to look and find it!

I think all human beings reach a point in their lives when they ask, 'Why?' 'What's my purpose?' 'What's this all about?' Some of us are good at pretending that we don't care, some of us cover this urge with material pleasures, some of us go down the wrong path, and some of us wait until we're on our deathbed before asking these fundamental questions.

I think these questions are part of our blueprint or DNA. We've all thought them at some point, but few of us do more than indulge in fleeting contemplation. But we should ask these questions to take us below our surface-thinking, to find the inner fulfilment and happiness that we are all seeking subconsciously. By having the courage and strength to search for the answers, we acquire higher wisdom and an enlightenment that shifts our consciousness – which, ultimately, helps us discover who we *really* are and therefore build our lives around our unique blueprint. When we do this we feel a tremendous sense of contentment, peace and harmony.

ARE YOU READY TO DIG DEEPER?

What I have rapidly come to realize is that if we don't start to take control of our lives, someone else will do it for us! You can either make the change or wait for change to be shoved upon you. The choice is yours.

This book is about taking control: deciding what you want from life, and understanding and implementing new tools and techniques to turn your long-forgotten dream into reality and opening your mind to a whole new way of thinking.

GET READY TO MAKE A DIFFERENCE

Now it's all very well buying this book, but, let's be honest, it's not going to do much good if it sits on your bookshelf for the next six months gathering dust and dog hairs. So many people read self-help book after self-help book, and never implement the advice imparted to them. Or some might start using the techniques only to give up a few weeks later because of a lack of tangible results. We're all looking for a quick fix, we all want our fairy godmother to appear from a fluffy white cloud and magically make everything better. But I've got something very important to tell you:

You are your own fairy godmother.

You have a magic wand that can transform your life before your very eyes, but no one has ever bothered to tell you about it. You walk around every day with magic at your fingertips, yet you never use it. How ridiculous is that? Ask yourself this: if what I'm telling you is really true, what would you change in your life? Yes, of course you'd magic a million pounds into your bank account... who wouldn't? But, what else would you change? What else would you alter with a wave of your magic wand? Your career? The way you feel about yourself? Your appearance? Your house? Your partner? Your kids? I'm going to show you how to be your own fairy godmother. I'm going to show you where to find that magic wand and how to start using it. You have all the power you need, right now, to create whatever it is you want.

I know from experience that the hardest thing about making any kind of change is getting started, but you've done the hard bit – you've made the decision to find a new direction. All you need to do now is read each chapter of this book and follow any actions I set. I promise that by the time you finish reading this book you'll be eagerly waving your magic wand in all directions and seeing some amazing results.

SOME THINGS TO CONSIDER BEFORE YOU BEGIN YOUR JOURNEY

Create Time

It's important that you find the time to do the exercises in this book. The exercises aren't the sort of thing you can do while cooking the dinner or doing the ironing. They demand time and thought. Take into account your weekly schedule and work out when you can spend quality time alone. We're not talking hours here; 45 minutes a week will suffice.

Don't Rush

We spend our whole lives rushing about. If we're not rushing to work, we're rushing to the shops or for a hair appointment. I want to encourage you to slow down. There are eight chapters in this book, and I suggest that you complete one or two of them each week. But if it takes longer, that's OK, too. The key, of course, is not to fall into the trap of procrastination. As long as you are consistently moving forwards, there is no need to rush through each chapter. Absorb the content and move on when you're ready.

Research

Throughout this book I will introduce you to some new and unfamiliar tools and techniques. All the exercises have been created and put together from my own personal experience. They are techniques I have used myself and with my clients, and they have been of huge benefit. But feel free to research other methods; there are many authors out there who will share alternative ideas. Keep your mind open.

Create Your Support Team

When embarking on any personal journey it's always a good idea to get others involved. It's always nice, whether you're feeling a little wobbly or you've made a major breakthrough, to have someone to turn to, maybe your partner, your brother, your best friend or even a good life-coach. A good support team is invaluable – and crucial to your success.

MY REASONS FOR WRITING THIS BOOK

My objective in writing this book was simply to awaken you to who you really are, to give you a deeper awareness of self. When you achieve this you realize that you've spent most of your life sleep-walking – quite literally! This book takes you on a journey of self-discovery; I hope to change your perceptions and open you up to a whole new way of thinking, a whole new reality. And, by doing this, you become free to live the life you've always wanted.

I combine spiritual practices with practical self-help coaching tools to ensure you obtain the maximum benefit. I also encourage you not just to take my word for self-discovery, but to seek the words of other teachers as well.

Remember, there is no rush; only we put pressure on ourselves. You cannot plant a daffodil and demand that it blooms overnight, to do so would be unrealistic. It's the same when making changes in your own life. I encourage you to be patient. I promise if you initiate just a few of the exercises suggested in this book, you will notice huge changes in your life.

HOW THIS BOOKS WORKS

In the next eight chapters we will embark on a journey of self-discovery during which we will cover various topics. You need to read each chapter in turn and complete the exercises as you go along. You might want to read the whole book first and go back over the exercises afterwards. It's up to you. I suggest that you use a special notebook or journal in which to complete the exercises. You will also need somewhere you can keep everything together in one place. A cardboard folder will do. You may also wish to make notes in this book as well.

Here is what we'll cover throughout your journey.

Chapter 1 Taking Stock

In the first chapter I'll help you to take a clear look at what is currently happening in your life, and at what areas of your life really need to your attention right now.

Chapter 2 What Do You Really Want?

Here we complete one of the most exciting exercises in the book: I will assist you in setting three big, life-changing goals that will enhance your life ten-fold.

Chapter 3 What's Going On in Your Head?

In Chapter 3 we delve into the dark realms of your mind to discover what you believe about yourself and the world around you, and how this affects your life. I will share with you lots of practical tools that will help you re-programme your mind for success.

Chapter 4 A New Way of Thinking

In this chapter I will introduce you to a new way of viewing the world, and how you may apply this to help create the life of your dreams and achieve anything you set your mind to.

Chapter 5 Who You Really Are

In Chapter 5 we take some time to look at your individual blueprint, and I show you how to build a wonderful life around your values, passions and talents.

Chapter 6 Beyond Your Physical Self

I'll be stretching your thinking even further in Chapter 6, as we move beyond the mind and body into the mysterious world of spirit.

Chapter 7 The Real Secrets of Making It Happen

This chapter is where the real action begins; I give you all the best-kept secrets, tools and techniques to help you make your goals and dreams become real.

Chapter 8 Facing Your Fears

Fear is one of the biggest things that stop us achieving success in life, so, in this final chapter, I will show you how to face your fears head-on to ensure that you never again let fear stop you achieving what you want.

Homeplay

You'll notice at the end of each chapter there's a 'Homeplay' section. These are specific action steps related to the chapter that will help you embed any new learning and also gain further insight. It's a good idea to complete your 'Homeplay' actions before moving on to the next chapter.

MY JOB AS YOUR PERSONAL COACH

My job as a personal life-coach is unique and very special. My only objective is to ensure that my clients reach their goals, whatever they might be. My role is to give them undivided attention and support. The wonderful thing about my being your life-coach is that I am completely impartial, unbiased and neutral. I have no preconceptions or doubts about your ability to achieve your goals, unlike your family and friends. As much as our families and friends love us, they naturally have their own ideas about what we should and shouldn't, and can and can't, do, and this may stop us from moving forwards in life.

I have high expectations for all my clients and I expect them to achieve amazing things while working with me. Just because I am not working with you in person doesn't mean that your journey should be any less powerful or transformational. I want the very best for you, I believe in you and I know you can do it.

Just think... if every human being could live the life he or she truly wanted, in line with his or her true self and adding value to the human race in some way, the world would be a totally magnificent place for each and every one of us.

My job is, first, to help you to become clear about what you actually want from the rest of your life. Many of us don't even plan what we're eating for dinner that night, never mind what we want from the rest of our lives, so this must be the first step on your journey. I will help you to come face to face with the real you for the first time in your life, and I will assist you to move beyond any self-sabotaging behaviours or beliefs that are holding you back. I will help you to adopt a 'Yes, I can' attitude, and take on a far more positive outlook to life. And, in true life-coach style, I'll motivate and inspire you to take action. In short, I will give you all the tools and techniques you need to turn your life around.

OK, so sometimes you will curse me or want to throw this book out of the nearest window, but if you stay the distance I guarantee that you will have a sense of achievement and joy such as you haven't felt since you were a child and had just received a gold star from your teacher.

I get the greatest pleasure out of helping people to achieve their dreams; it's a feeling that money simply cannot buy, and I wouldn't change my job for the world. I love it. So I am here throughout this book (and beyond, if you wish) to help you create your perfect life.

YOUR COMMITMENT

Now, it's all very well me committing wholeheartedly to you, but what about you making a commitment to yourself? Let's get one thing clear: if you are not committed to the overall journey, both the good and bad, what's the point of starting out? No commitment, no change. If you want big things from life, you need to get committed, and now is the time to do so. If you are not dedicated you might as well close this book now and give it to someone else who is. Generally speaking, people who seek out a life-coach are completely ready and devoted to making life changes. Just because this is a book and I'm not physically present, that shouldn't alter your commitment one iota! You either want change or you don't.

I work with lots of different people who have all sorts of weird and wonderful goals. Some people achieve rapid results from day one; others are much slower off the mark. Some individuals make enormous changes, others quite small ones. Why so? It all boils down to one thing: commitment!

The key, of course, is ensuring that you set the right goals from the start; that way your commitment will be unshakeable until the end of your journey.

Ask yourself: on a scale of 1 to 10 (1 being 'not bothered', 10 being 'totally focused'): 'How committed am I to making some big changes to my life?'

If you've answered 5 or below, I suggest you close this book and come back to it in a few months' time. If your answer is 6 or above, you are ready to start your life-changing journey.

One last thing: when people hire me to help them achieve their goals, I ask them to sign a coaching agreement. This agreement states my commitment to my client and what I expect from him or her in return. This way we both know where we stand and there is no ambiguity. So, before we begin, let's do just that.

Our Coaching Agreement

I commit to giving you my total dedication, allegiance and focus. I believe in you completely and will support and encourage you fully. – *Louise Presley-Turner*

Now your bit:
I commit to reading this book and completing all the exercises outlined, working for a minimum of 45 minutes a week. I am willing to keep an open mind and try out new ideas and techniques, and I will keep going until I reach my goals.

Your signature _____

OK, I think we're almost ready.

Just One More Thing Before We Begin

Take hold of my hand, I'm right here with you... your journey begins as soon as you turn the page.

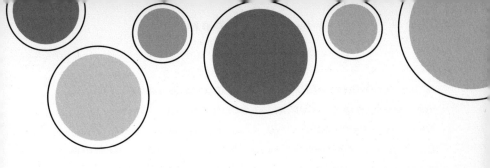

CHAPTER 1

Taking Stock

HAVE YOU EVER STOPPED TO ASK DIRECTIONS?

In this chapter I want you to take a snapshot of what is currently happening in your life. Before we can get to the exciting part of setting big, life-changing goals, it's essential that you look your life squarely in the face and be honest about what is – and what is *not* – working. As difficult as this may be, it's imperative that you do this before we move forwards.

No one really wants to admit that they've wasted 20 years of their lives in the wrong job, or that they've walked down the aisle with the wrong person, or spent three years training at university only to find out that they're in the wrong career. It's hard to swallow. But, difficult as it is, it's time to be wholeheartedly honest. Most of us spend years putting up with things that make us unhappy, never really getting to the bottom of our unease or understanding why we're feeling so unfulfilled. We pretend our lives are blissful, even though, deep down, we know they're not; we smile politely at the world around us, and run round and round our hamster wheel, repeating the same routines day in and day out. We suppress our real feelings until we're totally numb. Then we find ourselves jumping from one job to another, or from one relationship to the next, or we fill our lives with material pleasures that we believe will alleviate our pain and fill the void. None of these things works in the long run. No amount of shoes or DVDs will ever give our soul the inner fulfilment it so desperately seeks. But, because we are anaesthetized, we're oblivious to our own predicament; we just think it's normal. The years pass us by and nothing changes from one year to the next. And the story goes on.

So, how do you know when you're in need of a new direction? Here are some clues.

- You wish every day of the week away. When it's Monday you wish it was Tuesday. When it's Tuesday you wish it was Wednesday. In doing so you never actually live in or enjoy the moment.

- You watch far too much television, spend too much time on the phone gossiping with friends or searching through social networking websites to see what your mates are up to.

- When you get together with your friends all you do is moan about how bad your life is, and then end up feeling totally depressed by the end of the evening.

- You blame your bad upbringing, your poor education, the country, the economy or whatever for not having the life you want. You're a complete victim.

- You're envious of anyone who seems successful, and are quick to point out their faults, or find yourself saying, 'Oh well, it's OK for them...'

- You drink, smoke or shop too much as a way of making yourself feel better about your life.

- You only mix with people who are on your wavelength, as they're the only ones who really do understand what it's like to live your life.

- You always wake up feeling groggy and apathetic.

- You're always ill, catching every cold or virus going: this is just typical of your luck!

- You feel your circumstances are totally out of your control.

STOP THAT TREADMILL!

Let's face it, most of us are so busy gasping for the air we need just to get through each day that our dreams and goals are put on the back-burner for what seems like an eternity. The days fade into one long arduous week, and before we know it a year has vanished and we've gained yet another wrinkle. We've hardly had time to think about, let alone experience, our dreams and goals. We decide that this is how it must be for everyone because when we look around it appears that everyone is on the same treadmill. Others seem as hard-pressed, prodded, let-down and disappointed by life as we are.

Along comes another year: a time of new beginnings and positive action – a new season of promise and hope. 'This will be the year I change my life,' you hear yourself say. You convince yourself this year will be different, the year you finally lose that weight, start your own business, change career, get out of debt, find your life purpose or bag the man of your dreams. We muster all our ambition and positive energy into making this year the year that catapults us into a brand new, exciting life.

But many of us get caught up in the fast pace of modern living, as all those hopes and dreams quickly wither away and we're back to running at breakneck speed on our all too familiar treadmill. We resign ourselves to the notion that this is how it is: life's hard and we don't really have any control after all.

Modern living is just like a treadmill, never stopping, never ending. On and on it goes, and the constant grind over time takes its toll, not only emotionally but on your physical health, too.

In Western society we are conditioned to follow one another around, and I don't mean literally. I mean following past programming from generations gone by – from our family, teachers, friends and culture. In our society it's expected that you leave school, get a job or go to university and then get your first job, buy your first car, search frantically for Mr or Miss Right, buy a house, travel, have babies and, before you know it, create a trap of financial restraints and responsibilities for yourself. It becomes extremely hard for us to step off or stop that treadmill.

At school I really wanted to be a journalist because I enjoyed writing so much. In my final year I clearly remember having a meeting with my careers teacher to discuss my options. I had a few ideas about what I wanted to do – maybe an air hostess or working in the travel industry in some form or another – but what I really wanted to do was become a writer. I had struggled with most subjects at school, just about keeping my head above water. But I thoroughly enjoyed English; writing came easily to me and I was actually quite good at it, regularly getting the highest grades in my class.

As I sat in front of my teacher, young, naïve and simply looking for some sound guidance to point me in the right direction, her response to my ideas about becoming a writer was, 'You need to be realistic, Louise. To be a journalist you need to get "A" grades and then go on to university; have you thought about working with children?' Errrr, no! So there I was, a confused teenager out in the big wide world, what was I going to do with the rest of my life? I had no idea. Thankfully, I didn't follow my teacher's advice. I decided I would find my own direction. Unfortunately I didn't become a journalist, though; I ended up in a job in advertising, which wasn't a bad thing but it wasn't what I really wanted. It only took 12 years for me to realize this, so I suppose you could say my detour was relatively short in comparison with some. It wasn't until I started my coaching career that I finally put pen to paper.

Regrettably, when it comes to making career choices, many schools (and parents, for that matter) rarely look at a child's talents, capabilities, interests or passions. They tend to focus on what's logical and where the child would fit in or easily be placed. Many parents are happy to get their kids into a decent job earning a wage. This is understandable, but in doing so they miss something very vital and our children end up on the wrong career path, in occupations that simply aren't right for them. One woman client came to me having spent 20 years working in catering, even though she absolutely hated cooking. She told me that she was very creative, that she loved to sew and regularly designed clothes for herself or made curtains for friends and family. As a child she was excellent at sewing and arts and crafts and was told by her teachers she had a gift, a natural talent.

Her parents rarely took much notice of this and were more concerned that she achieved good grades at school. When she was 15 her family relocated from Scotland to Manchester, where her father enrolled her on a catering course at the local college. My client had no desire to build a career in the restaurant or catering industry, but it was what her mother had done all her life and she wasn't going to go against her parents' wishes. 'I was only 15, what did I know? I just did what I was told; I wanted to please my dad,' she explained to me. When she came to see me, she'd had enough of pretending to be happy, pretending that her life was OK; she wanted change, and a career that she enjoyed and that came easily to her. She had made a decision to transform her life and subsequently set herself a life-changing goal: to start her own dressmaking business. It only took her 20 years to realize that she was on the wrong path and do something about it.

The point I'm trying to make here is: how many of us really follow our dreams? How many of us, when we're at such a young and impressionable age, have the courage to go against the grain and do something different? Not many. It's so much easier to follow your dreams when you're young and naïve, and have energy and a passion for life. I'm not saying it's impossible as we get older, but it gets harder, that's all. It's no one's fault. We can't blame our parents for our job or the bad relationship we're in. Most parents simply do their best with their beliefs or state of consciousness. They know no different!

I want you to take notice of your treadmill. Are you really happy? Do you have a long-lost dream that somehow got shifted on to the back-burner? Maybe you've been doing the same job for years; it's comfortable but the days drag and you'd much rather be doing something else. Maybe you hop from job to job looking for the right one. Maybe you're stuck in a loveless relationship and are too scared to break free. Maybe you're a mother who is no longer satisfied with being everything to everyone else and having no time for yourself, or maybe, like I was, you're content in most areas of your life, but somewhere deep within you is a little voice that nudges you every time you start another week in a job you can't stand, or don't like what you see in the mirror, or you buy another Lottery ticket thinking money will solve all your problems. Do you hear a little voice that says 'Stop, there is another way'? Do you feel that something is missing, that you should be doing something else with your life? Each person's circumstances will be unique, but if you hear that inner call, feel that inner nudge, maybe it is time to start asking some deeper questions.

I wasn't even aware of my own 'rut' because I thought this was normal! Everyone around me was in the same situation and we were all on the same treadmill so I thought that that must be just the way it was. I never once considered that there might be another way. Why should I? We all have a 'comfort zone' inside ourselves where everything is safe, warm and stable. We have rituals and routines that we perform day in and day out and which keep us tucked nicely within our self-created comfort zones.

When was the last time you stopped to see where you were going? Did you check whether it was the right direction? Change is the single most important element in everyone's life, and only you can make changes to your life; only you can break free from the 'same old, same old...'!

If you live your life within the confines of your comfort zone, you are not giving yourself the opportunity to grow, to learn new things, be free, playful and spontaneous, and ultimately to enjoy a fulfilled life.

There's a very simple rule to consider: keep doing the same things and you'll keep getting the same things back. Give yourself permission to expand your awareness and stretch your invisible wings so you may fly a little higher and farther to see what else is out there. Who knows what you might find?

8

THE HUMAN CONDITION

Here we are: a supposedly intelligent species that split atoms and fly to the moon. Yet we humans still running around killing each other, dying of car letting half the world's population starve to de and ruining the planet with all our man-made tox Something has gone seriously amiss! This isn't h it's supposed to be, and deep down we all know it! all need to open our eyes.

We think that by straining, manipulatii controlling and forcing that we will have the abil to change the outward picture of our lives. We spe our whole lives trying to change the people around trying to change our current circumstances, workir our fingers to the bone just to make ends meet to buy the material things that we think will bring happiness. But if this were truly the answer then o world wouldn't be in the mess that it is.

We believe our lives are controlled by ou government, our boss, our partner, our neighbour. W honestly believe that we have no control because, 'It' their fault not mine; I'm just the victim.'

There's a world of 'closet sufferers' walking around out there smiling through their gritted teeth, who would swear blind that they are happy with their lot They'll tell you life is great, that they are totally happy and content. Yet these same people tell you life is hard, it's not fair that you just have to 'put up and shut up' and deal with whatever life throws at you.

I say, 'Rubbish! Life is not for enduring. Far from it, it's about living – living a fulfilled and happy life!'

Closet sufferers are just victims, plain and simple, viewing their world from their limited perspective. They honestly believe they have no control.

If I'm honest, I, too, was once one of those people, always blaming others for my misfortunes. On a Monday morning in the office you would find me standing over the photocopier, a cup of tea in one hand, a pile of unopened post in the other, gossiping about the events of the weekend or the latest addition to the team. Until my own journey began I was definitely a crowd-follower. Partly because I knew no different and partly because it was easier just to fit in that way.

Here's the truth of the matter: all change must start from within – this is the trick we're all missing! It's not the economy's fault that you're angry or dissatisfied, nor is it your boss's, your partner's or your neighbour's. I promise you, as long as you keep blaming all those around you, you will remain exactly where you currently are in your life. Nothing will change. YOU need to take responsibility for your life, starting right now.

We live our lives within the rules of society, our families and our culture – we have been told how to sit, how to behave, what to do. Until now, that is! Some people are starting to wake up and are trying to find that missing link in their lives.

There is a revolution afoot. Can you feel it?

Remember, keep doing the same things and you'll keep getting the same things back. Accept that

something is not working in your life – let go of the belief that you have no control.

It's time for us to stop being blinkered and insular, and to open our minds to new possibilities. In so doing we'll open doors into worlds we never knew existed.

STOP FOR A MINUTE AND BREATHE!

The thing that most people don't do is pause and take stock of their lives, and consider what makes them joyful and what makes them miserable. Sounds simple, doesn't it? But we just don't do it. Most of us spend our whole life hiding from our innermost feelings, following the crowd, travelling at breakneck speed and feeling depressed in the process. But, by doing so we fail to pick up the important messages that life gives us, and we need these in order to steer our lives in the right direction.

Many of the people who come to me have put up with undesirable circumstances for so many years that they have forgotten who they are: people who have been doing the same job for years even though they hate it intensely, people who have endured loveless relationships for far too long, those who have had serious money problems. The list goes on and on. Why do we let this happen?

The sooner we realize that something isn't working in our lives, the sooner we can do something about it instead of clinging on for dear life.

So, I want you to stop right now and take a deep breath. Dig out your journal and complete the following short exercise.

Exercise: Your Life Quiz

The following list represents eight main areas of your life. I want you to give each area a score between 0 and 10, 10 being perfection and 0 being awful. Take your time, but, most importantly, be honest with yourself.

Career	0	1	2	3	4	5	6	7	8	9	10
Money	0	1	2	3	4	5	6	7	8	9	10
Health	0	1	2	3	4	5	6	7	8	9	10
Family and friends	0	1	2	3	4	5	6	7	8	9	10
Partner/ romance	0	1	2	3	4	5	6	7	8	9	10
Fun	0	1	2	3	4	5	6	7	8	9	10
Personal development and growth	0	1	2	3	4	5	6	7	8	9	10
Physical environment	0	1	2	3	4	5	6	7	8	9	10

Once you have done this I want you to write down the three areas of your life that scored the lowest.

1 _____

2 _____

3 _____

Now answer the following questions.

- *What is currently making you most unhappy in your life?*

- *Why have you allowed this to happen?*

- *What will happen if you continue living in this way?*

- *How important is it that you make some changes (as a percentage, up to 100 per cent)?*

- *How committed you are to making these changes (as a percentage, up to 100 per cent)?*

This exercise plays a very important role in your journey to a better life. I will be referring back to this Life Quiz in later chapters, so keep it safe.

DON'T DRAIN MY ENERGY

For most people, as you've just found out, there are a few key areas where it is glaringly obvious that something has gone wrong and change is seriously needed. But, aside from the bigger aspects of our lives, there are also small things that we put up with that are relatively easy to change.

Think about your day-to-day life. If you're constantly looking at unfinished DIY, or if a cascade of clothes falls on your head each time you open your wardrobe doors, it's not going to help you in your quest for a happy life. It's going to drain your energy. I call these small things 'energy-drainers' because every time we see them they make us feel weary. Every time I look at an ever-increasing pile of ironing waiting to be done, or open my 'tax return' folder, my energy levels are drained until I feel disheartened and deflated.

What's the cure?

It's time to get rid of them.

Exercise: Banish Those Energy-drainers!

I want you to think of 20 things – people, circumstances or situations – that are sapping your energy. What do you have to do to eliminate them from your life forever? It might be the broken loo seat, the half-finished decorating, a killer commute to work or selfish friends who talk about themselves constantly.

Make a list of 20 things in your life that you are tolerating. Don't worry how small or how big these are – if they are draining your energy, write them down.

Now write 20 actions that will eliminate the items on this list forever – from paying your bills by direct debit to employing a cleaner, or having your grocery shopping delivered.

Here's the important part: lists are wonderful and I'm a huge advocate for them, but they're useless unless you can *cross things off them*. Pin your list where you cannot miss it and make a concerted effort to cross at least one thing off it each week. The satisfaction you'll feel will be well worth it and you will find you have lots more energy as a result!

YOUR HOMEPLAY THIS WEEK

- Pin your Life Quiz up on the wall, somewhere you'll be reminded of it daily.

- Start working your way through your 'energy drainers' list. Aim to eliminate at least two or three items over the next week.

CHAPTER 2

What Do You Really Want?

Congratulations, you've made it to Chapter 2! You've done the tricky bit in deciding which areas of your life need adjusting, and have arrived at one of the most exciting parts of the book.

It's time to be creative and start thinking big. You have now discovered what's not working in your life; it's time to understand what you *really* want. Sounds simple, doesn't it? Everyone knows what they want, right? Wrong!

Deciding what it is you really want and admitting it, not just to yourself but to others, is probably one of the most frightening and misunderstood undertakings in society today. Just thinking about turning your deep-seated, long-lost dreams into reality is far more frightening for most of us than having root canal treatment at the dentist's – without painkillers!

But, before we delve into the realms of 'What do I really want?' it's important to understand a few things. At this stage you're probably thinking 'I'm not going to start dreaming now. I'm 35, for God's sake; my life's all right, I've made do and I can't bear any more disappointment.' It's time to let go of this limiting thinking. We all see things we would like to have; we all have places we'd like to visit one day; we all have opportunities we should have taken. Sadly we've all been brainwashed into believing that wanting to live a bigger and better life is egotistical and selfish – but it really isn't. I believe we are all here to live our lives with purpose, and when we find our path we not only become happier, we make those around us happier, too. We are all here to add value in some way and make the world a better place in which to live.

Letting go of a lifetime's worth of programmed denial and disappointment can be terrifying, primarily because it means change. But change is exactly what this book is all about: *positive change*. And let go we must if we truly want to live a life that makes us feel fulfilled.

It's no wonder we're scared to dream any more. I'm sure we can all remember a time when we were very young, when we told our parents or siblings, 'I want to be a ballet dancer' or 'I want to be a pilot,' only to be told to stop fantasizing and concentrate on our schoolwork. We found out early in life that the more we wanted something, the more we experienced heartache. Even as toddlers who relished exploration we'd hear our mothers cry, 'Don't touch that!' as our tiny little chubby hands reached out for the best vase. Not just once, but time and time again: 'No, no, no, no, no!' By the time we reached our teenage years it was pretty hard to keep our dreams alive – beyond what was socially acceptable, of course: passing our driving test or buying our first house. Heaven forbid you should want to own your own company, drive a Ferrari or travel the world! Over time our dreams withered away, leaving us with maybe, just maybe, if we were lucky, a few small dreams – or should I say ideas; the ones we knew were achievable. And, I'm afraid to say, it's here we stay, many of us for decades, living our lives in our all-too-familiar, self-created comfort zone.

How depressing!

DREAMING BIG!

Now, when we are deciding what we really want it's important to point out that many people create dreams or goals based upon someone else's demands or opinions. I have clients who come to me saying, 'I want to do my degree because my father always wanted me to.' Or, 'I want to get a second job so I can pay for my daughter's riding lessons.' No! Your dreams should be about what *you* want, and not what someone else wants you to do. Living your life this way is futile and will, in the long run, deplete your energy and make you resentful. This is about you and only you! It's time to be selfish.

OK, so you'd like a bigger house, a fancy car, four holidays a year and, oh, a new sofa wouldn't go amiss – we all want these things. I want you to be more specific, get beneath the surface and dig *deep*. Living the life of your dreams has a lot to do with your values, passions and talents, and we'll discuss these in more detail later on. Of course, your dreams change over the years, and you've probably moved on from wanting the latest Action Man figure or a pair of black shiny tap-dancing shoes complete with satin shoelaces. Yet there is still within you an amazing inventory of long-forgotten fantasies. We all have old passions and long-lost dreams that we've put on the back-burner. It's now time to think again and move them to the front of your mind.

> *What do you really want? What are your most deep-seated dreams? Those which you find hard to admit even to yourself, let alone others. What are they? What are your most hidden desires, ideas and ambitions, things that you're too scared to dare even whisper out loud? Set your mind free and allow yourself to think big! Really big!*

I want you to forget that your dreams are 'too far-fetched' or that 'my friends will think I've gone bonkers' or that 'I'm not educated enough.' Forget all these things. Just because you've decided to make a dream your reality doesn't mean you having to explain your reasoning to your partner, mum, friends or even yourself. You deserve to live the life you want. Get rid of the notion that you have to be worthy or have to pass some test to qualify. It's rubbish. You're worth it! Other people will only water down your dreams, just as they always have done.

> *We arrived on this Earth to play, to create and, ultimately, to experience joy in the process. You have one decision to make – just one – and that is to decide to be happy.*

18

What is it that will make you smile from the inside out? The challenge is to peel the onion through layers of 'Should', 'Shouldn't' and 'No', and see what lies beneath.

One analogy would be: 'It's like holding a huge catalogue in your hand, and within it is every career, experience or dream you could possibly imagine having. Your job is to place your order.' How amazing would that be?! Well, it's time to start browsing.

MAKING THE DREAM REAL

I want you now to look back at the Life Quiz you completed in Chapter 1, and reconnect with the three main areas of your life in which you scored the least.

What we're about to do is the most important thing you'll ever do. You're about to create three life-changing goals that will transform your existence for the better. I want you to take your three lowest-scoring life areas and set one life-changing goal for each – that is, unless you already have a specific goal in mind. But, before you eagerly race off to do this, there are five things you need to keep in mind as you lay down your goals. These are:

1. Your goal must be *your* goal, not someone else's.

2. Your goal must be specific. Don't be too vague!

3. Your goal must be positive and inspire and motivate you.

4. Your goal must be achievable within a 12-month time span.

5. Your goal must be measurable in some way.

It's very important how you frame your goal, and the type of language you use. Let me explain.

Your Goal Must Excite You

All three of your goals should excite you. Now, I know from experience that when we set goals, although they may well excite us they also can scare the hell out of us at the same time. This is perfectly normal. Most people who experience a whiff of fear just curl up into a ball until the fear subsides.

What they fail to realize is that fear is just a normal part of life, which comes into play when we extend the boundaries of our comfort zones. We must embrace fear and not run away from it. Every successful person has felt fear at some point. They might not have called it 'fear', but I promise you they definitely experienced some discomfort on their journey to success. Period!

Remember, a good goal should both excite and scare you, at the same time. The idea is that your goals should feel uncomfortable, because if they don't then they are probably too easy! We'll discuss how to tackle fear in far greater depth in the final chapter.

Your Goal Must Be Positive

What you also want to avoid is setting goals that use negative terminology. For example, let's say you want to lose two stone in weight; you might decide that your goal is 'Finally, to be thin'. Think about this for a second: what does this goal imply? First, by wanting to be thin you are implying you are currently not, and, secondly, by using the word 'finally' you are subconsciously saying that you've tried many times before to be thin, and have failed. Can you see what I'm getting at? Every time you read this goal to yourself, you're likely to feel discouraged and apathetic rather than excited! Not a good start. A better way of putting this might be: 'To buy a pair of size 12 jeans'. Now that conjures up much better mental images than the first one. It creates a vision of being happy with your body image.

Let me give you some examples of both good and bad goal-setting.

Example 1

- To start my new photography business by January (good goal-setting).

- To get out of my current job and become a photographer (bad goal-setting).

Example 2

- To meet Mr Right by the end of the year (good goal-setting).

- Not to feel lonely any more (bad goal-setting).

Example 3

- To find a career that utilizes my skills and talents (good goal-setting).

- To stop feeling so bored and unfulfilled (bad goal-setting).

Your Goal Must Be Specific

Another important aspect to goal-setting is not to be too vague. Your goals must be specific; if not, how will you know if you've achieved them? Putting a deadline such as 'by January' or 'by the spring' really gives your goal some depth and accountability. Now, I understand that some goals are long-term ones, and may take a few years, but if a goal is set too far in the future it's extremely hard to keep motivated and on track. If it is a long-term goal, just break it down into small chunks and make sure that whatever target you set is achievable within a 12-month time-span.

Your Goal Must Be Measurable

Lastly, measurability is extremely important as it gives you a start and a finish point. Without some way of measuring your goals, or your successes, how on Earth will you know if you've achieved them? For example, can you measure your success in weight, money or level of happiness or confidence? Make sure you have some way of gauging your accomplishments!

FIRST STEPS

OK, I think we are all set to take the first step towards your new life. Here's the question: what are your three goals going to be?

What most people tend to find when setting their three goals is that they have one or two bigger goals and one smaller goal. That's perfectly normal. If you're still finding it difficult to decide what your goals should be, the following exercise should help to inspire you.

Exercise

- *Did you ever have a childhood dream? If so, what was it?*

- *Is there anything you're naturally good at, or that you find comes easily to you?*

- *What do you love to do in your spare time?*

- *Is there anything you're passionate about in life?*

- *If you had no limitations, such as lack of money or education, what would you love to do?*

- *What long-lost dreams have you been putting on the back-burner for the past five, 10 or 15 years?*

- *What is currently missing from your life?*

- *Is there anything you've seen or heard on TV, in a magazine or maybe from a friend or colleague that sparked some interest for you recently? What was it?*

- *What's the one thing you want to do before you die?*

- *What goals might you set that could make the biggest difference to your life?*

Having worked with many people who have set all sorts of life-changing goals, from business-related to personal or spiritual goals, I have compiled a list of genuine goals which my clients have set, just to get your juices flowing:

- To set up my llama-trekking farm by next April

- To launch my coffee shop and have a champagne party to celebrate

- To pass my bike test and organize a charity run before my fortieth birthday

- To move to Australia within 12 months

- To work abroad in an animal rescue centre

- To turn £10 into £1,000 by this time next year

- To design and build my own house

- To reach spiritual enlightenment

- To release my album

- To take on my first paying client

- To be featured in a national magazine

- To get to know 'me' better

- To climb to the top of Mount Kilimanjaro and raise money for charity

- To reach my target weight

- To wake up every morning with a smile on my face

- To pay £20,000 from my mortgage within one year and become financially FREE

- To have a turnover in excess of £150,000 by June

- To complete my first book and get it published before my baby is born

- To take up tennis again and start competing by the end of the year

- To go to Africa and work as a volunteer for Save the Children

- To start my own business.

This is it – time to create your life-changing goals.

Exercise

Write down your three goals here or in your journal.

Goal 1 _____

Goal 2 _____

Goal 3 _____

Still Stuck?

If you're still having trouble defining your goal or goals – stop. Put this book down, shut your journal and do something else. There is no rush. Go for a walk, play with the kids, have a cup of tea, do the ironing. Take your mind off it for a while. No one is demanding that you decide here and now, so don't put pressure on yourself. Take a break and come back to it later. What you'll find is that when you're cooking dinner or are in the shower, an idea will pop into your head. When it does, jot it down as soon as you can. You can't force inspiration; like a baby, it arrives when it's ready.

Once you have listed your three life-enhancing goals, I want you to complete the following exercise, which involves asking yourself four very important questions.

Exercise

1. *Is this really my goal?*

2. *Am I committed to achieving this goal?*

3. *Does this goal excite me?*

4. *Will achieving this goal make me feel happy?*

What you're looking for here is a resounding 'Yes' in answer to all four questions. If you don't hear it, ask yourself why. If you have decided on a particular goal because your partner thinks it's a good idea, it will not work. If you have set a goal you're not committed to, it will not work. If you've set a goal that doesn't inspire or motivate you, it will not work. And, finally, if achieving your goal won't make you happy, what's the point?

You know, deep down, when you've set the right goals because they *feel* right. If you're pondering too much then you haven't set the right goal, so move on to something else.

How Do I Know If I've Set the Right Goals?

- *You feel extremely excited and scared at the same time.*
- *You feel like jumping up and down on the spot.*
- *You feel impatient and immediately start researching your goals.*

- *You wake up in the morning and, maybe for the first time in years, you have a big smile on your face.*
- *You phone your mum, sister, brother or friends to share your overwhelming excitement.*

Colour Your Goals

Now I want you to do something extremely important. I want you to go and get a blank piece of paper and write down your three goals clearly and concisely. Do them in different colours: colour them in, make them stand out.

Once you have done this, go and pin your goals sheet where you will see it every single day: on the bathroom mirror, the fridge door or on your computer screen. It really doesn't matter where, but I want you to ensure that you will see your goals every day, so consider carefully.

PEERING INTO THE BLACK HOLE

I'm now going to do something rather odd. I'm going to take you into your own personal abyss (only for a few minutes, you'll be pleased to hear). I'm not one for negativity, as it's a huge energy-drainer, but there's a rationale behind this next exercise, honest!

I want you to imagine what your life will be like if you don't come out of denial and make some positive changes. Imagine 12 months have passed, you've totally forgotten about this little book and it's now tucked away on a shelf somewhere gathering dust, and nothing in your life has really changed. You're in the same position you are in today. You're still driving the same journey to work, you're still sitting at the same desk, looking at the same computer screen, you're still broke by the tenth of the month and, deplorably, you're still feeling unhappy and dissatisfied. You get the picture? Nothing has moved forwards. How will you be feeling? Stagnant, depressed, miserable, disheartened, frustrated, angry, unfulfilled, disgruntled and stuck in the same old rut.

Ask yourself: 'What will happen if I do nothing to change my life?'

Not a pretty thought.

Hey! Let's stop here. Enough is enough. I'm just trying to get you to see that life without change is the same as deciding that everything will remain the same. So, are you ready to make some changes to your life and make this the year that catapults you forwards into a brand new reality?

There is a reason why you're reading this book. Somewhere deep inside you, you want change. You want a better life, and you hear the ever-so-quiet whispers inside that are nudging you forwards. The time is now; the time has come for you to take control and start really living! Are you ready to experience what your life will be like when you've achieved your goals?

SEEING YOUR NEW LIFE IN FULL COLOUR

In order to help keep you focused and excited about your goals, I want you to create a future vision of your life once you have actually achieved them. Visualization is used by some very successful people, from authors to businesspeople, from entrepreneurs to Olympic athletes. Almost all athletes play their events through in their minds before the real thing. They feel the muscles they will use, how each one will tense and how much power is behind a jump or a sprint.

Every successful person will tell you the same thing: they could see their success long before it happened.

I remember deciding that I didn't want to work in advertising and marketing any longer. I was fed up with sitting in the same office, with the same people, doing the same work year in and year out, while my daughter was at nursery being cared for by someone else. I wanted more freedom, more passion, and I wanted to stop wishing my life away from one weekend to the next. I had no idea what I wanted to do at the time.

All I knew was that I wanted to do something worthwhile, something that made a difference to the world and something that would fit around motherhood while earning me the money I needed to sustain my standard of living. I remember that each night, before I went to sleep, I would spend a few minutes imagining how I wanted my life to be. I would envisage two years in the future and note all the changes that had taken place during that time. I could see myself with two small children. I could see my vegetable garden lush with marrows, carrots, potatoes and the like. I could see how wonderful my home looked with all the improvements we'd made. I could see as a family we were financially secure, and I could see myself running a business from home that fitted perfectly around my family life, giving me the freedom I desired. Every time I visualized and imagined how I wanted my life to be, I'd feel an overwhelming sense of peace and happiness, and I'd drift off to sleep with ease. I still do this exercise even to this day, and I always will, because it feels so good! Little did I know when I started doing this that, very slowly but surely, one by one, these things I'd imagined would start to manifest in my life. I did start to grow my own organic vegetables. We did make vast improvements to our home. Our savings did expand nicely and I did create my own business, working from home as a life-coach and writer. I had created exactly what I had imagined in my mind's eye.

> *Just 15 minutes of creative visualization a day can change your life in unimaginable ways. It's just that most people don't believe in the power of their own imagination. Do not underestimate this magical power.*

There has been extensive research into visualization and the power of intention. We'll be delving into this in more depth later on.

Enough about me and my vision, it's time to start creating yours!

If you're a non-visual person or have difficultly holding images in your mind, simply write your vision down on a piece of paper, or even create a 'vision board' full of pictures cut from magazines that represent how you want your future to look.

OK, ready?

Exercise

Make sure you are comfortable and won't be disturbed for at least the next 5 minutes. Take 30 seconds or so to relax and breathe in and out deeply. When you feel ready, close your eyes and begin visualizing your future reality as if it's already manifested. If you're non-visual, write down the answers to the questions below instead. Imagine you have moved into the future and have now achieved all your goals and dreams.

- *In this vision of your future self, when you first open your eyes in the morning and the first glimpse of sunlight is gleaming in through your window, what do you see?*

- *When you get out of bed and look out the window, what is the weather like?*

- *Whom do you share your life with and how do you feel about them? How do you behave around each other?*

- *What are you wearing/how do you look, and how do you feel about yourself?*

- *How do you spend your mornings?*

- *How do you spend your afternoons?*

- *How do you spend your evenings, and with whom?*

- *How are you feeling about your life?*

- *Look back over the previous 12 months and marvel at all the wonderful things you have achieved. Feel the feelings of success, satisfaction and fulfilment at just how perfect your life is now you've achieved your dreams.*

Daydream in this way for as long you feel comfortable and, when you're ready, bring your awareness back to the present, wiggle your toes, take a deep breath and smile.

You've just taken the first step towards making your goals a reality! Not only are you, on one level, helping to attract your goals, but on a very basic level visualizing keeps your dreams alive: it keeps the passion and enthusiasm burning inside you, and that's what you need if you want to turn your life around. I'd like you to commit to spending five minutes doing this exercise every day, maybe in the shower when getting ready for work or maybe in the evening just before you go to bed.

YOUR HOMEPLAY THIS WEEK

- Allow yourself to think big and decide on three goals that will change your life for the better.

- If you need a little inspiration, get outside, go for a walk and let the ideas flow.

- Make sure your goals excite you and that you are committed to them.

- Seek out people who have achieved similar goals to you; a great way to show you it can be done.

- Spend a few minutes every day visualizing what your life will look like once you have achieved your goals.

CHAPTER 3

What's Going On in Your Head?

So now you have created three exciting goals – *and* displayed them somewhere you'll see them every day. What next?

Before we start getting into physical action we still have some work to do, and by this I mean 'inner work'. I want you to put your goals to one side for a moment. I'm not talking about forgetting them; on the contrary, I'll be showing you later on the secret of how to make your dreams into reality. But before we breathe life into your goals, we have some very important topics to cover which will help you not only achieve your goals but also manifest a wonderful existence for the rest of your life. I want to talk to you about your *programming*.

Changing your life for the better starts by changing what you believe is possible.

Here's what is probably running through your mind right now: 'I think my goals are great in theory, but I can't see how on Earth this book is going to help me to achieve them, it's impossible' or 'It's nice to dream, but it isn't going to happen' or 'I haven't got time to do this.'

Sound familiar?

I've been there. I understand. But it's only a change in perception that is needed in order for you to achieve your goals.

YOUR FAULTY PROGRAMMING

We come into this world with a wonderful, individual, unique blueprint that holds within it our personality, talents, passions and values. It is these things which make us who we are. There are people who have natural talents for making people laugh, for healing or for nature. There are people who have natural talents for creating inspiring works of art, for playing musical instruments or for being able to sing in tune effortlessly. It's these differences which make our world such a diverse place in which to live. Thank goodness! We wouldn't all want to fancy the same person or pursue the same dreams in life. Imagine!

Although we each have our unique blueprint, there is a part of our brain that is untouched and open to programming. From very early on in life we are consistently creating new habits, beliefs and behaviours which become 'hard-wired' into our subconscious mind. In fact, it has been said that almost all our beliefs, habits and behaviours are created before the age of seven. Yes, really!

I like to think of the brain as a jelly: every impression made by our parents, siblings, teachers, nation, religion and culture leaves its mark in some way. And sometimes these impressions may mask our unique blueprint.

For example, when a toddler first learns to walk, it takes some time to master the skill and get balancing just right. Each time the child falls and gets back up to try again, he or she is creating a new neural pathway in the brain. Eventually, when the child finally conquers the art of putting one foot in front of the other, the neural pathway is hard-wired into the brain and walking becomes a habit and is therefore effortless. The child can walk without having to think about it. Think back to when you were learning to drive a car, or learning to read: very difficult at first, but eventually these skills became habitual.

Our understanding of ourselves and the world around us is created and hard-wired in exactly the same way. So, what are beliefs? A set of (perhaps rash) generalizations made – about others, about life in general and about ourselves. They form our version of reality, based on what we feel and perceive about our experiences. What you think and believe will affect the way you behave and perform, and influence the actions you take; they will shape your life as you know it.

So let's go back to the concept of the jelly. Our parents' beliefs are generally passed down to us. They pass on these beliefs in order to protect us (so they hope). Maybe you were discouraged from pursuing a particular talent because your parents thought you ought to be doing something more practical. Or perhaps as a young child you observed your siblings getting more positive attention than you did and therefore formed the belief that somehow you weren't good enough. Or maybe your parents constantly told you how unsafe the outside world was so that you formed a belief that we live in a dangerous world.

All these kinds of beliefs are destructive interpretations of ourselves and the world around us; they lie within our subconscious mind and we're not even aware that they exist.

Now, here's the really fascinating part:

> *The beliefs we create are not based on fact. They are simply opinions. There is never any hard evidence to support them. But, amazingly, we build our lives around these beliefs every day, because we think they are facts. They become the foundation for what we experience in our adult life.*

If, as a child, you were constantly told that money was tight, you may keep a tight hold on your money as an adult, or end up frittering away every penny at every opportunity. If you were told never to trust anyone, you'll spend your life watching your back and being suspicious of people. If you were told you weren't clever enough at school, you'll live your adult life thinking you're inferior or not quite good enough. Can you see what I'm getting at?

> *Here's the truly startling part: once we have formed a belief, we will continue to live our lives by it. We'll continue to find evidence to support*

our way of thinking – and will actively exist any challenges to our belief.

Think about it for a second. Your brain is consistently showing you evidence to support your belief, even though it's not fact! And your brain will instantly dismiss anything that contradicts that belief. Perhaps someone genuinely pays you a lovely compliment and you dismiss it by saying, 'Oh, it was nothing. Anyway, it wasn't really my doing.' Your underlying belief is telling you not to accept the compliment because it doesn't fit with your belief and therefore must be untrue.

If you were told as a child that you were ugly or fat, or that your brother or sister was more attractive than you, you quickly formed a belief that 'I'm fat' or 'I'm ugly,' and that belief is hard-wired into the brain. The brain's job is then to reinforce that belief by showing you evidence to support it in your day-to-day life. It might be that every time you look in the mirror your focus goes directly to your nose, your flat chest or your big bum. You will pick out what you consider to be your faults and dismiss any of the good bits. Now, remember, thinking that you are fat or ugly is just a belief, it's not fact! It is something you were told, that you decided was true and was therefore worth believing. The problem is that you take this belief into your adult life and it affects everything you do. It affects your confidence and your self-esteem. It affects the people you mix with and where you go. In short, it affects your whole life! Now can you see how destructive a limiting belief may be?

It's the same with money, love, education, health, career, family and so on. You need to become aware of what you believe about yourself and your world. We all become very good at finding evidence to support our beliefs, and we do this subconsciously – without question. Why? And how does this happen? It is because of what biological psychology calls the 'reticular activating system' (RAS).

The RAS is a collection of brain cells that acts like a radar system triggered by our beliefs. The RAS filters in information that is consistent with what we believe, and filters out anything that does not support our opinions.

Our 'results' are backed up by self-talk such as 'I knew that was going to happen,' 'That's just my luck' and 'I'm not good enough to do that.'

Together, our RAS and our self-talk form a comfort zone which represents the confines of our ability, based on our beliefs.

A simple exercise to demonstrate this theory: try to spot how many people are walking down the street wearing a red top. Having spent time counting people who are wearing red tops, try and remember how many other people were wearing green tops. The chances are you won't remember how many green tops you saw. You know there were some, but your attention was drawn to spotting red tops only. You can see just how powerful the mind really is. You must remember that your brain is a wonderful entity, and that *you* have the power to 'programme' it, consciously, whichever way you want.

Most of the beliefs you hold within you serve you well, and will continue to serve you well for the rest of your days. The problem arises when you allow limiting beliefs from the past to guide your present and future decisions. These negative beliefs will stop you achieving your true potential.

I believe that limiting beliefs are the biggest barrier to us achieving success in our lives. Limiting beliefs keep us trapped in our comfort zone; they keep us on the treadmill. In order for you to achieve your goals, you're going to need to become aware of any self-limiting beliefs that could potentially get in your way and sabotage your success.

LET'S BLAME THE PARENTS!

You are not responsible for the way you were raised, but you *are* responsible for what you do now. The past is past, you can't change it, so don't get hung up on trying to pin the blame on your parents, siblings, teachers, or anyone else for that matter.

Ignorance is bliss. Your parents can't teach you something they were not aware of themselves. Instead, try visualizing them as small, young, defenceless children themselves. See them with their little chubby faces, looking all innocent and helpless; now, think about where they grew up, the type of childhood they had, their parents. Where do you think their limiting beliefs came from?

Please don't blame anyone for the beliefs you hold. They are no one's fault, and channeling your energy into blaming others won't serve you well. It will just make you bitter, and that certainly won't help you move forwards on your path of self-discovery.

This book is about *you taking control of your life now*. Here – and now – is where your power lies.

SOME COMMON LIMITING BELIEFS

I have listed some of the most common limiting beliefs I have encountered in my life-coaching practice. As you read through the list, ask yourself if you believe any of them (or a variation of them) and, if you do, ask yourself why you believe them.

- I'm not clever enough.
- I'm not educated enough.
- I have no special talent.
- I'm not attractive enough.
- I'm not strong enough.
- I'm not gifted.
- It always works for everyone else, but not for me.
- There's a finite amount of money I can earn.
- Bad things always happen to me.
- I never win anything.
- Nobody likes me.
- I'm talentless.
- Rich people are untrustworthy and selfish.
- Life's hard.

- I can't trust anyone.

- This world is a dangerous place.

- I am always getting ill.

- I have a slow metabolism and that's why I'm overweight.

I'm not one for delving into the past to find out why. Yes, it is important to uncover a limiting belief and maybe find out where it originated, but nothing more. All we need to know is *what our limiting beliefs are*: from there we have the power to do something about them. As I've said before, no one is to blame for them, and raking over the past really doesn't serve you well. It may be more destructive than the limiting belief itself.

Here's the good news: *you can change a limiting belief*.

Hooray, that's a relief isn't it?! Let me explain. Just because a neural pathway has been created and hard-wired doesn't mean it can't be 'rewired'. Think of your brain as a mass of circuits and connections: just as you can rewire your house, you can rewire your brain.

Here's a good example. When someone has a stroke, normally the lack of oxygen to the brain means that in certain areas the neural pathways die away. It tends to affect the speech or the ability to walk, read or write, and so on. So, arguably, stroke patients almost regress to being children in some ways. They then have to start the process of having to learn to talk, walk, read or write again. And the amazing thing is that they do! Of course it takes time, but they start forming new connections in the brain, and eventually master the skills once more. My point here is that you have the ability to change a belief, a habit or even a behavioural pattern, even if you've been running it for the last 20, 30 or even 50 years of your life.

Remember, your brain is like an incredible bio-computer; all you need to do is install the right software and watch the magic unfold.

But before we get to the exciting bit about how to change a belief, I want to talk to you about your habits and 'behavioural masks'.

WHAT ARE YOUR BEHAVIOURAL MASKS?

'What's a behavioural mask?' I hear you ask. Well, the only way I can describe a behavioural mask is as an overcoat or hat that we decide to put on when we interact with the world around us. When a particularly strong negative belief takes hold of us, we create a behavioural mask that we put on subconsciously. It's like a protective barrier which covers up our true self.

For example, if, when you were a child, you lived in a large family and the only time you ever got any attention was when you had a problem or were hurt, you probably formed the belief that 'to be loved I must have a problem.'

It was a good way to get attention, and when you got that attention you received the love you so needed and craved. So, how does this translate into your adult life? In order to get attention as a child you created a behavioural mask to get your needs met, and even though 30 or so years have now passed, you are still acting out that same behaviour pattern. Have you ever met a hypochondriac or someone who always seems to have one problem after another? Have you ever wondered why he or she acts in this way?

Although this type of behaviour may be very effective at getting our needs met when we are children, by the time we reach adulthood it is outdated and can cause us lots of problems. Nobody really wants to spend time with someone who is very needy or who has lots of problems. In fact, acting this way will have the opposite effect. To start with people will want to help you, and they will do everything they can, but eventually they will get fed up with you whining and whingeing, and will leave you, which – of course – just backs up your original belief that you are not worthy of attention. It's a vicious circle. I'm not saying that everyone who holds this type of belief will act in this way; it's just an example. But what I am saying is that, as human beings, we do tend to create some odd habits and behaviours in order to compensate for our unmet needs and act out our limiting beliefs.

Once you can identify that you are wearing a behavioural mask, or even a few different masks, you can decide whether they are serving you well or not. Although it can be a very liberating experience, it may be extremely uncomfortable to discover a particular behavioural mask you've been using for many years. It can feel like someone has stolen all your clothes and you're running around naked trying to find them. But, don't worry, this book is about self-discovery, and

that means peeling off all the layers, one by one, that you've acquired over the years, and discovering who you really are! Behaviour is just another layer.

One important thing to remember is that beneath each of the masks listed below lies a limiting belief of some description. See if you can work out what the belief might be for each one.

Are you ready to have a look at some typical masks?

The Poseur

This is the type of person who likes to be centre of attention all the time. They're only truly happy when everyone is looking at them. They hate being on their own and are generally quite loud and flamboyant.

The Superhero

These people are always running around helping people and playing the 'hero'. They get more joy out of helping others than they do out of helping themselves. They're always busy doing something for someone else; they never get time for themselves. In fact, they just seem to attract people into their lives who need help.

The Bullshitter

They are always telling wild stories about their amazing lives. They like to boast about their so-called accomplishments and often find themselves lying in

order to look good, and end up in all sorts of tricky predicaments. They have no real substance, and people never know when they're being honest.

The Comedian

This person is always joking around and playing daft tricks on people. They're always the ones who crack the first joke, they struggle to be serious for long and find it difficult to be around solemn people.

The Dizzy Blonde

We all know the person who always says daft things and comes across as generally unworldly, almost a bit dim. They are even sometimes referred to, these days, as 'a bit blonde'. They're always looking for someone to rescue them and take responsibility.

The Bully

This is the type of person who comes across as very intimidating. They like to be heard, and don't like anyone who opposes their decisions. They're generally very loud and belligerent, and they like to be the centre of attention.

The Pessimist

These people believe 'it's too good to be true' or 'it'll never last.' They never trust anyone and are always cynical. Their glass is always half-empty and they find the negative in any situation.

The Anarchist

They like to be different, to go against the grain. They hate any type of authority – like the boss, tax inspector, traffic warden or police.

The Injured Party

These are the type of people who are always in some kind of crisis. Something bad is always happening to them, whether they are being sacked, breaking up with their partner yet again, bumping their car or simply having a bad day.

The Speed Demon

These people never sit down for longer than five minutes. They are always rushing around, generally because they have left everything to the last minute.

The Obsessive

Obsessives like to do everything themselves because only they know best. They are perfectionists; it's not right unless it's done exactly the way they like it.

The Sex God/dess

Terrible flirts. They like to know that people around them are attracted to them. They enjoy seducing people but, once they know they've got someone in the palm of their hand, they lose interest.

The Chameleon

These are the people who change their personality or voice to suit the situation they're in. If they're talking to someone who is well off, they'll mention the fact they drive a Mercedes; if they're talking to someone less affluent they'll adapt their story, telling him or her how much in debt they are. They are constantly changing their life story in order to fit in.

WHAT ARE YOUR MASKS?

There you have it, behavioural masks revealed! So, which one (or ones) fit you?

Exercise

Write down your top three behavioural masks and the underlying belief you think you're compensating for. (For example, 'I always play the "sex goddess" because it feeds me with the love I'm craving and makes me feel esteemed and appreciated.')

Mask 1 _____

_____

Limiting belief causing mask is _____

_____

Mask 2 _____

_____

Limiting belief causing mask is _____

_____

Mask 3 _____

_____

Limiting belief causing mask is _____

_____

Yes, it can be quite hard to come to terms with the fact that you've been hiding behind a particular behavioural mask for most of your life. But it may be cathartic and healing at the same time. If you want to find out who you really are, and what you really want, you first need to know what subconscious behaviours you are creating in your daily life.

When I first uncovered my behavioural masks (and yes, there was more than one), I felt like someone had stripped me of my personality. Remember, though, it's not your *real* personality you're letting go of, but behaviour you've created as a result of a limiting belief you hold.

The real you is someone who isn't trying to be someone they're not; you're not performing or bending yourself into some bizarre outward appearance in order to try and impress people, or fit in with the crowd. You will be yourself, saying what you really think. Can you imagine how nice it would be to be your true self? To be less false, less tense and completely comfortable with yourself – probably for the first time in your life?

One point I'd like to make here is that when we start to change a behavioural pattern that we've been running for a long time, those around us will be a bit concerned or confused: 'Why aren't you flirting with me any more?', 'Why have you stopped cracking so many jokes?', 'Why aren't you joining in with the Monday morning gossip?' Don't let this deter you: you can't be something you're not just to please someone else. Remember, this is *your* journey.

LET'S REWIRE THE HOUSE!

Now, it's all very well uncovering your behavioural masks, but you can't really drop them until you address what the limiting belief behind each mask actually is, and that's what we're going to be doing next. Once you can change a limiting belief for a healthier one, your behaviour will change automatically. Having looked at your limiting beliefs and behavioural patterns, the next step is to decide to change a particular belief or behaviour that is limiting you in some way. Start with one belief at a time; you can move on to any others later on. It's a bit like going to the gym in January. You're raring to go; you can see the benefits of getting fit and are desperate to start seeing results immediately. If you are anything like me, you start off by going five times a week, but by the second week you've dropped down to four times, by the third week you're going twice and by the end of January you've stopped going altogether. When introducing a new habit or routine into your life, don't make it too hard for yourself or you'll run out of steam far too quickly and give up! Be kind to yourself, there's no rush. It has taken you all your life to get where you are now, so don't expect things to change overnight.

Try this: fold your arms in front of you, the way you would normally fold them. Come on, fold your arms; it'll only take a second! Are they folded? Now notice how familiar and comfortable it feels. Now, unfold your arms and fold them the opposite way. Can you feel how unnatural and strange it feels? If I were to tell you that from now on you could only fold your arms in this 'new' way, it would take a certain amount of time and effort before it became habitual. It's simply because your brain likes to follow the same pattern, and when you try to change or introduce something new, it protests.

You need a degree of commitment and time when deciding to change a limiting belief or behaviour pattern. Without your commitment, nothing will change. Many of us think that just because we've uncovered a limiting belief or a less than desirable behavioural pattern, somehow that is enough. It's not! You need to take some physical action in order to change any aspect of your life.

Exercise Part 1

Make it your intention to start noticing the beliefs of those around you. Notice the things people say in their general conversation. If you listen carefully, you'll be able to hear their personal beliefs seeping through. Observe your partner, your children, your hairdresser, your friends, your boss, the check-out woman at the supermarket. Study the language of pessimistic people and of those who seem to have a sunnier disposition. It's very interesting!

The reason I'm asking you to do this is because it's far easier to notice the language, habits and behaviours of others than it is to observe our own.

Do this exercise for at least one week. You'll be amazed at what you discover.

Exercise Part 2

I want you to get your own beliefs clear now. Everyone has hundreds of different beliefs, some good and some bad, but no doubt you'll have a few fundamental ones that have really shaped your life as you know it. Take 20 minutes to do a 'mind dump' on a large blank piece of paper, listing all your beliefs about every aspect of your life – both big and small. I want you to think of the beliefs you hold in the areas of your life listed below.

Write as many good and bad beliefs as you can think of, concerning:

- *relationships*

- *work or career*

- *personal image*

- *personality*

- *health*

- *finances*

- *the way you see the world.*

Now use your 'mind dump' to devise two separate lists, one of all the negative beliefs and one of all the positive beliefs you hold. Once you have done this, look at your negative list and underline the three beliefs that are having the most impact on your life ('I never have enough money,' 'I'm unattractive,' 'I'll never find a job I'm happy in,' for example).

List your top three limiting beliefs below.

Limiting belief 1 _____

Limiting belief 2 _____

Limiting belief 3 _____

Exercise Part 3

Now answer the following questions for each of your three negative beliefs. It's important that you understand the impact your negative beliefs are having on your life.

- In what way is this belief unfounded or untrue?

- Where did this belief come from (your mother, your teacher, your best friend)?

- How has this belief limited you in your life so far?

- What does holding this belief cost you on a daily, weekly or monthly basis?

- What will happen if you continue to hold this belief?

Can you see what impact your limiting beliefs are having on your life? Remember, each and every day you are living your life by the rules of the beliefs you hold – isn't it about time you dropped the ones that hold you back?

Once you have revealed the top three limiting beliefs you'd like to work on, and looked at the impact they are currently having, ask yourself, 'Am I ready and committed to changing these beliefs?' If you're not, ask yourself, 'How are these beliefs and behaviours serving me?'

When you feel committed and ready to move on, the next step in the process is consciously to choose to create new, healthier beliefs to replace the old ones: beliefs that will help you to expand, to grow and, ultimately, move out of your comfort zone to live a bigger and better life.

Creating a new belief is extremely simple. It's really a case of stating the opposite to your limiting belief, as demonstrated here:

- 'I'm not clever enough' will become '*I am clever enough to achieve what I want in life.*'

- 'I'm not gifted/educated enough' becomes '*I have many gifts.*'

- 'I have no special talent' becomes '*I have many hidden talents.*'

- 'I'm not attractive enough' becomes '*I am attractive in many ways.*'

- 'I'm not strong enough' becomes '*I am physically and emotionally strong.*'

- 'It always works for everyone else but not for me' becomes '*There is no reason it can't work for me.*'

- 'There's a finite amount of money I can earn' becomes *'There is abundance in the world for me.'*

- 'Bad things always happen to me' will become *'Good things happen to me all the time.'*

- 'I never win anything' becomes *'I am open to winning things.'*

- 'Nobody likes me' becomes *'There are a lot of people who enjoy my company.'*

- 'Rich people are untrustworthy and selfish' becomes *'Rich people are the same as everyone else: some good, some bad.'*

- 'Life's hard' becomes *'Life has many joys.'*

- 'I can't trust anyone' becomes *'There are a lot of people in my life whom I can trust.'*

- 'This world is a dangerous place' becomes *'This world is a safe place for me to live in.'*

- 'I am always getting ill' becomes *'Every day I feel healthier and healthier.'*

- 'I have a slow metabolism and that's why I'm overweight' becomes *'I love my slim, healthy body.'*

Exercise Part 4

Looking at the three limiting beliefs you listed above, work out what your top three new beliefs need to be ('Money is now flowing freely into my life,' 'I am attractive,' 'I am working in my perfect job,' for example).

New belief 1 _____

New belief 2 _____

New belief 3 _____

How will adopting each of these new beliefs change your life?

New belief 1 will _____

New belief 2 will _____

New belief 3 will _____

Now, I know you're probably sitting there thinking, 'Well, this is all very nice, but I don't believe these new beliefs.' Hang fire! Rome wasn't built in a day, so stop being impatient!

When you first create a new belief, it may not seem true – and I know this because I've been there. Your new beliefs may seem, to you, to fly in the face of 'reality'. But think of each of your new beliefs as a small seed. You and I both know that seeds don't just develop and bloom overnight, even with help from Miracle-Gro® plant food! What we're talking about here is creating a brand new neural pathway in the brain, and doing this will take time. Remember the earlier arm-folding exercise? And if you're wondering how long it will take, unfortunately I can't tell you: it all depends on you and how committed you are.

Below I have outlined four ways to re-programme your subconscious mind with a new belief. There are lots of different ways of doing this, but I have come up with what I have found to be the most successful methods:

1. Creating evidence
2. Affirmations
3. Visualization
4. Self-hypnosis.

Let's take each one and break it down.

CREATING EVIDENCE

Like its name suggests, this method entails writing a list of evidence to support your new belief. What I mean by this is creating a list of things, situations, events and conversations which back up or prove that your new belief is true. This will help to form a new pathway in the brain. For example, if your old limiting belief was 'I'm unattractive' and you have decided that your new belief is 'I am attractive,' your list of evidence would include things like compliments you have received from people, or times in your life when you've felt at your best, maybe your wedding day or 21st birthday. You're simply listing evidence that will support your new belief. So sit down and give yourself an hour or so; really think about it. Go somewhere quiet where you can escape the normal pressures of life. You might find it difficult to think of things at first, but keep going; once you get into the swing of it you'll find that the evidence will start to flow. If you find it really hard, then keep coming back to your list over a couple of days. One of my clients went through her diary at the end of each week and wrote down all her accomplishments – from walking the dog, mowing the lawn and meeting someone new, to winning new business.

Once you've created your list, you then need to add to it continually, each time a new piece of evidence presents itself. It's really important that you refer to your list often – preferably daily. Not only will this help you to see that your old beliefs are simply unfounded, it will help create that new, much-needed pathway in your brain.

For me, I put my evidence list in my Filofax because I know I will have to open it every day and my evidence will fall out, which in turn prompts me to read it. Perhaps a bedside table or the fridge door is best for you – anywhere you cannot miss it. You might even put it in a shoe – it all depends on how serious you are!

AFFIRMATIONS

Affirmations are nothing new and have been well publicized over the years. By affirmations I mean repeatedly saying your new belief to yourself, over and over again, either out loud or in your head. This might sound a little odd to begin with, but it has been proven that saying or writing down your new beliefs is an excellent way to create a new pathway in the brain. For example, if your new belief is 'I am attractive,' you could commit to saying this 10 or 15 times in a row, three times a day. It might sound like quite a chore, but don't be put off; there are lots of ways you can do this. It's also important to point out that you don't actually have to say your affirmations out loud; you can always do so in your head, which of course makes it easier depending on where you are. I tend to chant my affirmations in the car, because I'm normally alone and can say them as loudly as I want to. You might repeat your affirmations in the shower, in the bath, when you go running, before you go to sleep, before you get out of bed, when you're ironing, washing or gardening – the list is endless. When you really think about it there are plenty of opportunities throughout your day to integrate this new routine.

The most important thing is to put some emotion behind the affirmations. Feel what it actually feels like to be living that affirmation. Without the emotional connection, your affirmations won't be effective. It's vital for your affirmations to become part of your routine in order for them to work – just like cleaning your teeth. If you find chanting your affirmations a bit dull, how about singing them? Make it fun, not monotonous. Think, what would work best for you? One of my clients created a list of the new beliefs that she wanted to work on and then produced a recording of her own voice on her MP3 player. She would then listen to the recording while she was cooking, ironing and even before she went to bed.

Another really powerful way to do your affirmation is to stand in front of a mirror while you're saying them. It is important to keep your affirmation in the present tense and avoid the use of negative words.

Good examples include 'Money is now flowing freely into my life,' 'The world is a safe place for me to live in' or perhaps 'I have lots of friends who enjoy my company.'

You may find that writing your new beliefs down works best for you. By this I mean writing your belief on a piece of paper (Post-it® notes are great for this). You might even write your belief down on a blank piece of paper 20 times in a row, similar to doing lines at school. For me the best thing is to write my new belief on numerous Post-it® notes and then plaster them all over the house! Well, almost all over: I tend to keep most of them upstairs so the only people who see them are me, my family and my friends. New beliefs tend to raise a few eyebrows! Put them around the bathroom mirror, on the bedside table, inside the wardrobe door, in a personal organizer, on your bank statements and on your computer screen: anywhere where you know you can't miss them. One client even wrote her new belief in red lipstick right across her bathroom mirror!

What's interesting about doing this is that, since both your conscious and subconscious mind will be picking up these messages, communication is working on two levels.

VISUALIZATION

Now let's look at visualization. Visualization (or using your imagination) is something we've already covered briefly in Chapter 2, but let me expand a little further here. As I mentioned in Chapter 2, visualization is a powerful tool used by the world's most successful people. It works on the same principle as the methods we've just discussed and is great at creating new neural pathways in the brain. I use visualization as part of my daily routine – not only to conquer limiting beliefs but for many other things as well. The great thing about visualizing is that it's relaxing and energizing; in fact, it's addictive! It's also extremely simple and everyone has the ability to do it.

Close your eyes for 5 minutes and create a vivid image in your mind's eye of your new belief being part of your life, almost like looking at yourself six months from now, whether that involves enjoying better health, having more confidence, meeting a new lover or finding a fabulous new job. While visualizing, remember to use vivid images, sounds and smells to make your mental images as real as possible. Be careful not to let any unconstructive thoughts creep in, keep it positive!

Once you have created your vision of your new belief, you can call it up any time you like. Great times for this are just before you go to sleep or when you are in the shower. You'll be amazed at how powerful it can be when done regularly.

SELF-HYPNOSIS

I'm a massive fan of self-hypnosis and have been using it for many years to help me change my mindset and achieve my goals. There is no doubt in my mind that my success so far is largely attributable to this wonderful practice. Self-hypnosis can be used for just about any kind of self-improvement as well as for reducing or eliminating physical symptoms or medical problems. During hypnosis, suggestions are given and accepted as being true, and these then affect our beliefs, habits and perceptions. It's a fabulous way to change your negative beliefs and imbed new ones. A good way to start is by using self-hypnosis audio tapes. There's lots of choice out there, on numerous different topics such as confidence, money, relationships, health and so on. Find one that resonates with you and start listening. I always listen to mine on my MP3 player just before going to bed each night, as I find that's when I'm most relaxed. For best results you need to use it every day, for a period of at least 30 days.

WHAT WORKS FOR YOU

So there you have it. Does one of these methods resonate with you? Which one are you willing to try? Maybe you'd like to create your own unique way. It doesn't really matter; you just need to decide what will work for you.

Perhaps you should try each one in turn, or how about trying all four together? Remember, be kind to yourself and give yourself time. Keep your mind firmly locked on the future, not the past, because that's where your power lies!

DO YOU HEAR VOICES?

To help you further on your journey to revealing your limiting beliefs, I want to introduce you to two characters in your life. I say 'introduce', but you're probably already very well acquainted. These two characters are with you at all times, morning, noon and night. They are with you at every success and every failure, at every crossroads and with every decision you have ever made, or will ever make, in your life, good or bad.

Ultimately, listening to one character will direct you to the life of your dreams, whereas the other will have you running around in circles and getting nowhere fast.

I call these two characters your 'Inner Guide' and your 'Inner Critic' but, quite frankly, you can call them whatever you fancy: 'Angel and Devil', 'Light and Dark', 'Tom and Jerry' or even 'Luke Skywalker and Darth Vader'. Identifying the different voices and scripts between these two characters is paramount in helping you to understand your internal dialogue and, eventually, your own limiting beliefs.

Your Inner Critic is loud and aggressive. This is the voice that consistently tells you how stupid you are, how unattractive you are or how unlucky you are. This voice was formed early in childhood as a tool of protection and its job was (and still is) to keep you safe and cosy within your comfort zone, keeping you from any potential harm. For example, if you were bullied at school, your Inner Critic will have formulated the belief 'Don't be different or you'll get picked on'; its job would then be to make sure you lived your life in line with this particular belief so that you wouldn't get hurt again. Your Inner Critic simply does its job. It keeps you tied to the confines of your beliefs, finding 'evidence' along the way to support them. The problem is, as we grow up our Inner Critic is still trying to rule us, even though we have outgrown the beliefs that were formed in our childhood.

Living life ruled by our Inner Critic is a recipe for disaster as it prevents us from moving outside our comfort zone. Unfortunately, most of us live our lives governed by this voice alone, simply because no one has ever told us there is another way. But you'll be pleased to know there is a simple solution, which we'll come to just as soon as we've met the counterpart of the Inner Critic – your 'Inner Guide'.

Your Inner Guide is quite different from your Inner Critic. The bad news about the Inner Guide is that this character is very softly spoken, so its whispers may be very difficult to hear over the much louder and more aggressive voice of the Inner Critic.

Your Inner Guide comes right from within, from a higher wisdom of knowing which I call 'gut feeling' or 'intuition'. Once you start to listen to your Inner Guide instead of your Inner Critic, your life becomes transformed. The job of your Inner Guide is to keep you true to who you are and to your unique blueprint. It knows what will make you happy and it knows how to get you there – all you have to do is tune in and listen!

The Solution Is Simple: Start Listening!

Notice which voice is more prominent, and when. Do you find you are spending most of your day listening to your Inner Critic? Do you find that this voice is louder when you're in a particular place or with a certain person? If this is the case, it's a clear indication that behind this voice lies a limiting belief of some kind which needs changing. When you hear the negative drone of your Inner Critic, ask yourself 'What limiting belief is my Inner Critic protecting me from?'

Exercise

I want you now (in your journal or on a blank piece of paper) to characterize both your Inner Critic and your Inner Guide. I want you to describe what both characters are like. Is your Inner Guide like an angel? Is he or she dressed in casual jeans with a warm smile and a fresh face? Is your Inner Critic a wrinkled old woman with no teeth, or dressed like a traffic warden? Have fun with this. I'm just trying to help you to differentiate between the two characters, or voices, because when you do this, you're halfway there.

Now, answer the following questions.

<u>*My Inner Critic*</u>
- *What is the general conversation of your Inner Critic? (What type of things does he or she say to you?)*

- *When do you find your Inner Critic is loudest? (When I discuss money with my partner, when I'm in a meeting with my boss, when I look in the mirror.)*

- *How does this affect you? (Stops me from progressing in my career and becoming successful.)*

- *What steps can you put in place today to ensure you turn down the volume of your Inner Critic?*

My Inner Guide
- *What is the general conversation of your Inner Guide? (What type of things does he or she say to you?)*

- *When you feel like you have failed, what does your Inner Guide say to you?*

- *How can listening more to your Inner Guide change your life for the better?*

- *What steps can you put in place today to ensure that you start listening more to your Inner Guide?*

Make a decision today to start noticing which voice you're listening to. Is it your Inner Critic, keeping you in the confines of your own prison, or is it your Inner Guide, guiding you to your ultimate happiness?

Exercise

To learn to listen more carefully for your Inner Guide, for the best results make it a habit to sit in your favourite chair or lie on your bed and spend 5 minutes a day tuning in to your Inner Guide. What has it got to tell you? What is its advice? The more you can do this, the easier you'll find it to tune in to your Inner Guide at any time of the day, no matter what's going on around you.

Commit to doing this exercise for seven whole days (just 5 minutes, perhaps in the shower or before you get up or go to sleep) and make a note of any ideas or insights you receive during this time.

HOW MUCH DO YOU REALLY LIKE YOURSELF?

One thing I quickly came to realize when I started coaching clients was how little self-worth people actually have for themselves. Most people don't really like themselves at all.

Everything you attract into your life is a mirror of what you believe you deserve: jobs, people and circumstances are all reflections of how you feel about yourself. Just as with our limiting beliefs, our self-worth is created very early on in life by those around us. Having two young children myself, I'm very aware of the messages they receive and I'm constantly telling them how wonderful, clever, special and beautiful they are. This is quite different from the messages most of us received as youngsters. I want them both to have the highest degree of self-worth possible, because I know that if they truly love themselves they will never need look outside themselves to others to make them feel esteemed or appreciated.

When we dislike ourselves we are constantly looking for approval from friends, parents and lovers. I know fully grown adults who are still desperately seeking the approval of their parents! All approval should come from within and not from others; otherwise we spend our whole life desperately seeking endorsement from outside sources. Loving yourself isn't egotistical or big-headed, that's just a fallacy. Loving yourself is extremely healthy – and those who do live much more satisfied, peaceful lives than those who don't.

> *People who hold positive beliefs about themselves seem to attract more good into their lives: they enjoy more opportunities, love and success on their own terms, and are happier and kinder human beings altogether.*

Exercise

- *On a scale of 1 to 10 (1 being 'not very much' and 10 being 'very much'), how much do you like yourself?*

- *Why have you given yourself this score?*

- *Where did your beliefs about yourself originate?*

- *What gets in the way of you loving yourself more?*

- *What limits do you create by not loving yourself fully?*

I think it's fair to say that most of us have some kind of limiting belief about our self-worth; I certainly haven't met anyone who hasn't. But in the same way that you address a limiting belief using the methods we've talked about, you can also address your level of self-worth and take steps to increase your self-esteem and self-acceptance.

Here's one technique for you to try.

Exercise

Find some quiet time, just 5 or 10 minutes when you won't be disturbed, and stand in front of a large mirror and look at yourself face-on. Take a couple of deep breaths and relax.

I want you to look into your own eyes and tell yourself 'I really love you.' Notice how your body reacts to this message: you may feel the need to look away, you may even feel tearful or you may hear your Inner Critic dismiss this positive statement, replacing it with something negative. Doing this exercise can feel very odd and uncomfortable to begin with, because we spend our entire life scolding ourselves rather than using words of love and praise. By doing this exercise you are releasing old, negative beliefs and re-programming your mind with more positive messages that will enable you truly to love yourself.

Repeat the statement 'I really love you' enough times for you to be able to fully accept it. If 'I love you' is a push too far, you can repeat something like, 'I truly accept myself for who I am' or 'I am healthy and my body is filled with energy.'

I suggest you do this exercise for a few minutes every day; make it a habit, just like brushing your teeth, and notice the difference it makes over a month.

Exercise

- *Write down five things that you like about yourself.*

- *Write down three things about yourself for which you are grateful.*

Put your answers somewhere you will be reminded of them often!

LIFTING OFF THE LAYERS

Uncovering limiting beliefs really is just the first step on your journey to self-discovery, but, in my eyes, it's the most important part. You need to know what you believe about yourself and the world around you in order to point your life in the right direction. Take one step at a time. Challenge your beliefs. Peel off one layer at a time and that way it won't feel so uncomfortable. Just when you think you've cleared away one belief, another one will appear – but that's OK. Think of it as de-cluttering your house or weeding your garden: you may well have a mad blitz initially, but you know it's inevitable that you're going to have to keep on top of it. It's a never-ending journey. You need to keep de-cluttering and you need to keep weeding. Accept that it's all part of life's course, part of your unique journey. The more you let go of your limiting beliefs, the happier you'll become and the more true to yourself you will be. You'll have the courage, perhaps for the first time in your life, to experience new things, meet new people and create a life beyond your wildest dreams!

But it all depends on you. Nobody is responsible for your life but you, and once you really and truly accept this, you have won power back! With this power you will then have the ability to create miracles.

YOUR HOMEPLAY THIS WEEK

- Get clear about your beliefs, and pinpoint the three that are having the biggest negative effect on your life right now.

- Create your three brand new beliefs and pin them up somewhere you can see them.

- Create a ritual or routine for programming your mind with your new beliefs, from affirmations, visualization, evidence journaling or self-hypnosis.

- Start noticing which behavioural masks you're wearing and drop the ones you know aren't serving you.

- Start noticing your own internal dialogue, both negative and positive, and tune in to your Inner Guide on a daily basis.

CHAPTER 4

A New Way of Thinking

In this chapter I'd like to introduce you to a fascinating concept that will undoubtedly stretch your thinking further, taking you out of your comfort zone into unfamiliar territory. When I found out about this concept my life changed overnight, and things have never really been the same since. I want you to read this chapter with an open mind and heart, as what I'm about to share with you has the potential to change your life immediately in unimaginable ways.

YOUR HIDDEN POWER

What would you say if I told you there was a hidden power within you that had the potential to create a world you wanted to live in: a world of greater prosperity, happiness and peace? Would you think I had gone bonkers or was living in 'la-la land'?

Probably: I can't blame you if you did. But I can assure you I'm not bonkers and I am definitely not

71

living in 'la-la land'. In fact, my feet are well and truly rooted in the ground for the first time in my life.

I'm sharing this with you because once you discover this inner power it has the ability to change your life beyond belief – and I'm not being all 'airy-fairy' here. I mean it will change your life in unthinkable ways.

There is power running through your body, causing your heart to beat, your blood to flow, your cells to regenerate and your hair to grow. A life-force energy with such effect that all these things happen effortlessly and without our intervention. This immense power makes your life possible and enables you to read these words; it not only makes you tick, it makes all life possible, everywhere. In fact, this power is exactly what thrust this very book into your hands! This power is known as the 'Law of Attraction'.

This law, just like the law of gravity, has been around since the year dot. Only now is science starting to recognize and appreciate its importance, and hence publicize it to the world. As a consequence, many people are now waking up to this intriguing law and are instigating its principles into their lives.

I first stumbled upon the Law of Attraction after the birth of my daughter. A friend with whom I worked at the time came bouncing into my office early one Monday morning beaming from ear to ear. She produced a bright orange book from under her arm and shoved it into my hand with very little explanation, saying, 'You must read this!' I was a little bemused, to say the least, but promised her I would take a look.

This bright orange book sat unread on my kitchen work surface for almost three weeks before the obligation to my friend to read it made me pick it up. But within two chapters this book had not only captivated me, it had thrown my life upside-down (in a good way). It had turned my version of reality on its head and opened a door in my mind that had been locked shut since the day I was born. My life would never be the same again, and deep down I knew it – I had felt an enormous shift.

So what is the Law of Attraction, and what could possibly have had such a profound effect on my life? Well, let me begin by telling you what the Law of Attraction states:

> *Your thoughts and feelings create your reality – every thought you think, no matter how trivial you might believe it to be, has an impact on your world.*

Philosophers have been telling us this for thousands of years: what we think, we become. Science has proved that our thoughts and feelings really do create our reality. Let me repeat that:

> *Your thoughts and feelings create your day-to-day life, all the good and the bad. Nobody is responsible for your life but you!*

Most of us, however, rarely make the connection between the trend of our thoughts and the way our lives work, so when someone tells us the cause of our troubles is our own thinking, we brush it off as nonsense. But if you look hard, you can see it working not only in your own life but also in the lives of all those around you.

WE ARE ALWAYS CREATING!

Think about it! Everything you think about in your mind will eventually on some level become your reality.

Have you ever wondered why some people seem to 'have it all'? Happiness, money, love, the perfect job, freedom... What is it that they do differently from you? Consciously or unconsciously, they use the power of their thinking to shape their lives. I know for certain that changing your life by changing your mind works. I know, because I've done it. Whether you're devoutly religious, deeply spiritual, an atheist, agnostic or simply sceptical, the reason I became a life-coach is because I wanted you to know just what a powerful creator you are, and show you how to start using this power to your advantage.

YOU ARE A HUMAN MAGNET!

Let me explain further. Every thought you have vibrates at a certain frequency. It is then broadcast out into the universe and attracts all things that are vibrating at that same frequency. Therefore, whatever you give off simply comes back to you like a boomerang, whether it is good or bad. The truth is, every hour of every day we have the ability to create our lives the way we want them to be, from attracting our dream job to solving conflicts or our global pollution problems. We just need to realize that when we come together and unite we have the potential to change our world! No one lives beyond this Law just as no one lives beyond the law of gravity. It's just that, until recently, we never realized that it applies to you and me.

The Law is impersonal; it doesn't judge or punish you, it simply plays back to you what you send out. The law of gravity isn't personal; it doesn't decide one day it will work for you and next it won't – thank goodness! The Law of Attraction is no different, it's just energy doing 'its thing', doing what it has always done since the dawn of time. As I've said, no one lives beyond this Law and it is behind every success or failure in our lives. We are literally walking magnets, constantly attracting into our experience anything that is on our frequency.

Science is going through some remarkable changes at present as we continue to understand more about how the universe works. At the forefront of these exciting changes is quantum physics. In rudimentary terms, quantum physics is the study of small particles of energy. Now, I'm no scientist and therefore am not qualified to explain the inner workings of quantum mechanics, so I'm going to leave that to those who are far more qualified. All we really need is to learn how to apply this Law of Attraction to our everyday lives. I would argue that we don't really need to know the science behind the Law of Attraction. Just as I know that the house gets warm when I press the button on my central heating controller, without my having to understand the ins and outs of how my boiler works, I don't need to be a quantum physicist to be able to make the Law of Attraction work for me. For those of you who need a little dose of science to help you understand the concept, however, studying quantum physics will provide you with the answers.

OK, so let me ask you this: what is it you're *expecting* to happen in your meeting with your boss? What are you *expecting* the traffic to be like when dropping the kids off at school? What are you *expecting* to see when you look in the mirror? What are you *expecting* to see when you look at your bank statement? What you are *expecting* to happen in your life?

If your answer to these questions is 'The same as always,' I've made my point: this is the Law of Attraction being demonstrated in your life. If you think and believe the same things, day in and day out, you will continue to experience the same things in your life. You get what you expect!

Your thoughts are energy. And your life is like a holographic image of the thoughts and beliefs you hold in your head. The movie screen you call your life is created by the thoughts, feelings and beliefs that you hold in your mind. In your everyday natural state you have the ability to manoeuvre your life in the direction you want it to go, from having a happy fan life to influencing world peace, simply by changing your thoughts. And you change your thoughts by changing your feelings.

Let me explain. We actually create by means of our feelings, not our thoughts. If thoughts are the steering wheel, feelings are the engine that drives the car. We get what we get by the way we feel and not by trying to force things into place or by trying to control the mind. In short, it's not about monitoring every thought in our head (this would be impossible), it's simply about monitoring our feelings and emotions, as they are a clear indication of what we are thinking and, therefore, creating.

If you are worried about money you are sending those thoughts and feelings out into the universe, and the universe will match those vibrations and keep sending you more of the same – more money worries. Remember: the universe simply gives back what you send out. So it's essential you start to become aware of your dominant thoughts and feelings. It's not until you change your thoughts and feelings that your vibrations will change and, in turn, your circumstances will alter as a result. It's the same with your relationships with family and friends, your job, your health, your weight and so on.

When you are feeling happy and joyful you are sending out high-frequency vibrations, and you may be sure that you are attracting things you want and desire back into your life, hopefully the manifestation of your goals! On the flip-side, when you are feeling lousy and consumed with worry or fear you are sending out low-frequency vibrations, which are only going to bring the things you don't want in return. So, whether it's high vibrations of love or low vibrations of fear, whatever you're vibrating at any given moment is what you are attracting back into your life.

Have you ever experienced a day where things just seem to go from bad to worse? Perhaps you start off in the morning by having an argument with your partner and leave the house feeling angry and frustrated. You then get caught in horrendous traffic, so by the time you arrive at work you are really wound up, and from there the day just snowballs. Sound familiar? Why is this? The more sustained negative thoughts and feelings you have, the more highly charged emotions you are sending out into the universe. The universe responds to the vibrations you are giving off and returns more of the same. When I stub my toe or break a glass, it's a gentle reminder to stop and bring my attention to my thoughts. What am I thinking? What am I feeling right now? It's a reality check – it's the universe's way of saying, 'You're heading in the wrong direction, turn around!'

We need to wake up to the fact that we are not just flesh and bones, we are electro-magnetic beings – walking magnets able to attract into our lives whatever we desire by controlling the feelings that are generated from our thoughts.

THE MASS CONSCIOUSNESS

We live on a planet of predominantly low frequency, brought about by over six billion inhabitants who are all vibrating more feelings of stress, worry and fear than feelings of love, joy and peace. This is because most of us spend our entire day listening to our Inner Critic, whose job is to keep us confined to our limiting beliefs. This can make trying to raise our own frequencies or vibrations difficult. Sometimes we can feel down without really knowing why; this will usually be because we're picking up on someone else's negative energy or vibrations. We literally bathe ourselves in unconscious negativity, from things like watching distressing shows on TV, reading the newspapers and mixing with negative people. You know this is true when a negative person walks into a room and you immediately feel the difference in the atmosphere. Conversely, you also feel it when someone positive walks into the room, as you pick up on their positive vibes. We've all experienced this at one time or another.

Without a doubt, as we go about our daily lives we are picking up energy from those around us. I have made a vow to myself not to get mixed up in negative conversations or tittle-tattle, read certain news stories or gossip magazines, or even watch heavy or negative TV programmes because they affect my mood and the way I feel. It doesn't mean I don't care. On the contrary, it just means I try to keep to a minimum the outside circumstances or moods that will influence my own. This also means not getting involved in someone else's negativity. As much as you might think you're helping them, you are actually making it worse not only for yourself but for the other person as well. Of course, when a friend or family member is in need, we should step in and do all we can to help. The world would be a horrible place if we didn't help our fellow neighbour. But we must watch out for 'energy vampires': people who are perpetual pessimists and who consistently sap us dry.

Your life is like a blank canvas on which you may paint whatever picture you fancy. The problem is, no one has ever told you that you have complete freedom in choosing what to paint. So instead you look across at the person at your side and copy them. In doing so you find yourself painting with the same colours and drawing the same pictures over and over again, simply because you know no different. In truth, you actually have access to hundreds of colours and may paint whatever picture your heart desires. So ask yourself: 'Have I been painting the same picture over and over again?' Maybe now is the time to start painting something new.

The more people who know and understand about the Law of Attraction, the more we will begin to see a shift in the mass consciousness on our planet.

UNDERSTANDING AND TAKING RESPONSIBILITY

Take the very first step with the Law of Attraction: understanding. You need to understand and research. Don't take my word for it. Investigate and find out for yourself. On my own journey I have learned never to take one person's word as gospel. The truth lies within you, right now. It's just a case of finding the right people, teachers, books and workshops to help you to discover your own inner truth.

Once you fully understand the Law of Attraction, move on to responsibility. This is the hard bit, as you need to take responsibility for everything that has ever happened in your life – all the good and all the bad.

As you embark on this adventure, you soon realize that there are no victims in life. Playing the victim just guarantees unhappiness from the prolonged emission of low vibrations. Accepting liability can be extremely hard for people; some people just find it easier to blame others for their misfortunes. You must take responsibility in order to embrace the concept, and use it to your advantage. The rest of the world will continue to blame their partners, bosses, friends, governments and so on for what is happening in their lives, or will blame their circumstances for their bad luck, or even God for punishing them. Please don't judge anyone for coming to this conclusion. I remember being so excited by the realization that what we send out comes back to us and that we all have the potential to shape our lives exactly how we want – how amazing! It really felt like I had the missing key. But, naïvely, I expected everyone else to be as excited as I was. They weren't! In fact, they just shot me down, and told me I was being ridiculous and outlandish.

What I have come to realize is that people's consciousness evolves when they are fully ready to receive. When this will occur is down to the individual, and no amount of convincing or cajoling will change that one iota. We are each of us on our own path and exactly where we should be for our own evolution. Just because you might believe the Law of Attraction – or anything else, for that matter – don't expect everyone else to do the same, because they won't. This is your journey, so stop worrying about others and concentrate on yourself! Realization comes to everyone eventually.

Right now it's important to realize that no one's asking you to become a goody two shoes all of a sudden – skipping around smiling from ear to ear. Let's get real here. Some days are better than others. Life is about duality. You can't know light unless you know dark. You can't know cold without knowing warm. You can't know sad without knowing happy. This is what life is all about. Please don't expect that just because you know all about belief systems and the Law of Attraction that you're never going to experience another bad day. You will, I promise you! From time to time you will stub your toe, have a disagreement with your partner, scratch your car or break a nail. Life will sometimes throw us really difficult challenges. We cannot ignore the fact that people get cancer, people die, sometimes awful things happen. Understanding the Law of Attraction doesn't mean you're exempt from anything unpleasant happening to you; nor will it solve the world's problems overnight. It just means you become more self-aware of how you're thinking and feeling, and can pull yourself out of any unwanted emotions far more quickly than ever before. You can play your part in creating a happier world for yourself and others.

The Law is simple in concept, but practice is necessary to apply it effectively. Like everything you read in this (or any other) book, it will never do you any good until you actually integrate the techniques and advice into your life. It's not enough to 'know it', you have to 'live it' and practise it to understand it fully and see the evidence flow into your life.

THE MAGIC OF 'FEELINGS'

If you don't have what you want in your life right now, you will probably find that it's because you are consistently thinking about what it is you *don't* want, and are spending most of your day listening to your Inner Critic. 'I don't want to be in debt,' 'I don't want to be in this relationship,' 'I don't want to live here any more,' 'I don't want to be unhappy,' 'I don't like my boss,' 'I don't want to be overweight,' 'I don't want to be ill.' I call it the 'I don't want' syndrome. Remember, the Law of Attraction takes your predominant thoughts and feelings and gives you more of what you're thinking about. The thing is, an awful lot of our thinking is done at a subconscious level and we aren't even aware of it. Most people will swear blind that they never have any negative thoughts whatsoever, yet these are the same people who constantly moan about the weather, the government or the number of speed cameras on the roads, and so on. We have over 60,000 thoughts a day; I wonder how many of those we are actually aware of? Let's be honest, you're never going to be able to monitor 60,000 thoughts a day – it would drive you insane! This is why it's extremely important to become aware of how you're actually *feeling*. Your feelings tell you what you're thinking, and therefore what you're attracting into your life.

Let me repeat that, because it's important: your emotions tell you what you're thinking and therefore what you're attracting, and they are the most valuable and powerful tool you have in your life.

It's pretty easy: mastering your feelings is the key to attracting what you want in your life. Your feelings are your gift from above to help you to steer your life in the right direction. Think about it for a second; it's really simple: your feelings tell you, at any given moment, what you're attracting into your experience. Isn't that amazing?! You don't have to worry about monitoring every single thought that comes into your head; you just have to be aware of how you're feeling at any given moment. This is where your Inner Guide comes in: he or she is there to assist you in raising your vibrations by helping you to change the way you feel. Feeling good means you're attracting what you want into your life. Feeling bad means you're attracting what you don't want.

So ask yourself now: 'How do I feel?' 'Who am I listening to at the moment, my Inner Critic or my Inner Guide?'

Are you feeling good? Are you feeling bad?

It all starts with awareness, and by asking yourself 'How am I feeling right now?' you have taken the very first steps in organizing the future you want. You are the one with all the power and you need to start believing it! You have the ability to change your life, because you are the one who chooses your thoughts and feelings every second of every day. No one can do this for you. You are in control. You are in the driving seat.

Remember: you are your own fairy godmother!

It's a bit like realizing that all of your life you've been driving a car without knowing where you want it to take you. You've just done what you thought you ought to be doing, pootling along and hoping you end up somewhere lovely. Finding out about the Law of Attraction is like being given the missing directions, except that these directions are really simple. It states: *Follow your feeling and the universe will direct you to your desired destination via the fastest and most harmonious route. Ignore your feelings and the universe will take you on all sorts of detours, moving you farther and farther away from your desired destination. It's imperative to get clear about where you're heading and what your short-term and long-term goals are.*

HOW DO I CHANGE THE WAY I FEEL?

If someone at work upsets you, it shouldn't affect the way you feel for the rest of the day. Yes, for a few minutes maybe, but not all day. It's the same with anything: getting a parking ticket, having an argument with your partner, finding out you're overdrawn at the bank, spilling red wine down your favourite white trousers or being let down for a date. By letting something – or someone – drag you down for longer than it or they should, you are throwing power away, and at that point you have stopped steering your 'life car' in the direction you wish to go. Don't do it, don't give your power away!

I'm not saying we should deny all bad feelings; that would be unrealistic. We need to experience negative emotions as much as we need to experience positive ones. As stated earlier, life is about duality; we need to know light to know dark, and hot to know cold. But when you do find yourself feeling down, change your mood by changing your thinking. Don't stay in a negative place for longer than you need to, because it's just bringing you more of the things you don't want.

It's also important to point out that just because someone has embarked on a spiritual journey doesn't mean they won't get fed up from time to time. Come on! We're living a human experience, and yes we'll have good days and bad days, and yes sometimes people will irritate us. Life is about making our experience as pleasurable as possible. We can achieve this, first, by monitoring our thoughts and feelings.

So don't beat yourself up if you experience negative emotions, they are part of being human. Take them as a signal that you need to change your mood, and tune in to your Inner Guide. How do you change your mood? Well, it's unique for every individual. You need to find what works for you. What you're looking for is something which will shift your thinking away from the unwanted situation and change the way you're feeling in an instant. I call these 'mood-shifters'. They may perhaps be a secret list of things to help put you back on track when you're feeling negative or downbeat.

Exercise

Create a list of mood-shifters that you think will work best for you. Write your list in your journal or on a blank piece of paper, and when you're feeling down refer to it to lift you back up again. Here is a sample list to aid your thinking:

- *Past memories, for instance of your childhood, wedding day, holidays*

- *Your children and funny things they say and do*

- *Your family pets*

- *Your home, your garden*

- *Special events that are coming up*

- *Special places you like to go*

- *People you love*

- *Your favourite music*

- *Nature*

- *Your favourite hobby or pastime.*

When I first started doing this I remember typing and laminating a list of all my mood-shifters, and when I found myself feeling less than happy I would go and sit in the Ladies' (at work mainly), read through my list, close my eyes and think about each one for a few seconds – it worked wonders for me! Some days I found myself sitting there quite a lot and other days less so.

You need to find what works for you. It might seem like too much effort to begin with, but believe me it's not – and, more importantly, it is worth it! It becomes second nature and, as we outlined earlier, it's just a matter of re-programming the mind. So yes, at first it feels a little odd, but within a matter of weeks or months you'll be changing any unwanted negative emotions into positive ones in a jiffy.

Another exercise to try is to programme your day in advance. Instead of letting the day control you, why not take hold of the controls and create the sort of day you would like to experience instead?

Exercise

Do this each morning before you start your day. It takes only a couple of minutes and can be done while you're in the shower or getting dressed.

- *Find somewhere you can relax, perhaps a favourite chair or on your bed. Make yourself comfortable and start breathing in and out deeply until you feel your body relax. When you're ready, close your eyes.*

- *Take note of all the wonderful things you already have in your life, from your comfortable home, friends, family, your health or your material possessions. Note everything for which you're grateful, big or small. Leave nothing out!*

- *Now, imagine another 'you' standing in front of you. This is your true self, the real you! Now notice how your authentic self stands, talks and moves. Notice the confidence that oozes out of your true self and how relaxed and comfortable your other self is.*

- *Imagine stepping into your true self's body, so your two bodies now become one. Notice the difference it makes to your confidence and the way that you feel.*

- *Visualize carrying out your day living in the body of your true self: today you are going to be the real you! See yourself doing all your normal activities and talking to your family, friends and colleagues. See how wonderful your day is and how smoothly it runs. Notice how confident you are and how happy you feel. Take a couple of minutes to plan exactly how you want your day to go.*

- *Open your eyes and slowly bring your awareness back to your surroundings. Don't forget, have a wonderful day!*

THE POWER OF APPRECIATION

Appreciation is another great tool to help lift those good old vibrations. Being grateful will guarantee that you bring more wonderful things into your life. I remember first finding out about 'appreciation' and thinking 'How on Earth can I feel appreciation for something that I don't like?' But I was missing an important lesson. Without feeling appreciation, or gratitude, for the things you currently have in your life, you fail to live in the moment. In fact, you miss it completely. Feeling appreciation is the most powerful way to make yourself feel better in the moment. So before you start your day, thank the heavens for exactly where you are in your life, thank the heavens for manifesting more good into your life, thank the heavens for the day ahead, thank the heavens for the people with whom you will share your day, thank the heavens for the food on your plate, for the car you drive, your children, your partner, your job and so on. The list goes on and on. We all have things to be thankful for. Each and every one of us! Feeling appreciation naturally raises your vibrations without you really having to think about it. If you get stuck finding things to be grateful for, ask your Inner Guide for help.

> Be grateful for what you have now, and start looking at the world through different eyes, through the eyes of appreciation. Appreciate the beauty of Nature, appreciate your family, appreciate your company for paying your wages, appreciate life and – more than anything – appreciate you for being you, as you are unique and there is simply no one else like you. Nobody does you better!

Since I started my own journey of self-discovery, cultivating my beliefs and practising the Law of Attraction daily, the one thing that has changed is my ability to appreciate my life fully. Whereas before I was always the first to find the negative in a situation, now I'm the first to notice the beauty. I am utterly grateful for everything in my life. I haven't necessarily got everything I could possibly want or desire, but I am grateful for what I currently have, and not a day goes by when I don't thank heaven for all the wonderful things

I have in my experience: my children, my husband, my family and friends, my beautiful home, my garden, the town in which I live, my car, my daughter's school, my local shops, the supermarket delivery man, the food in my fridge, my wardrobe, my cosy bed, my lovely warm pyjamas. And that's just the tip of the iceberg. There is no end of things to be thankful for in anyone's life.

I recently spent the weekend at a health farm (Christmas present from the family!) and I was sitting contentedly by myself in the restaurant having my breakfast. While I was there, three middle-aged women came and sat at the table next to me. Within seconds I could hear them moaning about the dirty tablecloth and that one of the seats felt wet. I glanced down at my tablecloth: mine looked perfectly clean. I then heard one of the women complaining that the restaurant had only brown bread, not white (bearing in mind they had come in 10 minutes before the end of breakfast service). Then the same woman chastised the waitress for taking her (empty) plate away before she had finished eating. Their conversation was just a barrage of negativity. As I sat there I couldn't believe what I was hearing. Here we all were, at this beautiful spa, being waited on hand and foot when others in the world are dying of hunger, and this woman couldn't see just how blessed she was. So what if there was a mark on the tablecloth or if there was only brown bread? It wasn't the end of the world! Remember, you get what you believe, so the more this woman picked up on things that dissatisfied her, the more things she started to notice and complain about. Change your perspective and you can find a million things, every day, for which to be grateful.

Being grateful is just a skill we can all learn. Just like re-programming our limiting beliefs, we can programme ourselves to be more appreciative of the things we have in our lives.

Exercise

Create a daily gratitude journal, where each morning or evening you list ten things you appreciate about your life. Your list might look something like this:

- *I appreciate the gorgeous sunshine today.*

- *I appreciate Mum's help with the kids today.*

- *I appreciate my boss for paying my wages.*

- *I appreciate this book for helping me on my journey.*

- *I appreciate my cosy warm bed.*

- *I appreciate my reliable car.*

- *I appreciate my hubby for making the dinner.*

- *I appreciate the supermarket delivery man.*

Keeping a journal really highlights the good in your life, and as a result you start to become a more positive person, always looking for the good! It works!

WHAT IF NOTHING SEEMS TO CHANGE MY MOOD?

If, for whatever reason, you find yourself completely immersed in negativity and you really can't shift from the pessimistic place in which you've found yourself, I have a trick up my sleeve.

Energy wants to move because in its natural state that's what energy does – it moves. When you feel negative it is because you are retaining energy that wants to travel in and out of your body. Your body doesn't want to retain energy; its job is to act as a conduit through which energy flows. It's only when you stop energy from passing through your body that you create all sorts of problems for yourself, including physical ailments; this is why stress is such a killer! We stop energy in this way unconsciously. By prolonging negative thoughts and feelings, we simply stop the energy from moving. The more we hold on to negative thoughts and feelings, the more the energy builds up and the worse we feel. Sometimes people suppress negative energy, such as guilt, anger or an inability to forgive, for years and years, but at some point the energy must be released: it will resurface, and may do so in one of many forms. Sometimes it resurfaces at the most inopportune moment, perhaps when we meet a new potential partner or when we start a new job. In the worst-case scenario, prolonged retention of negative energy may even manifest as serious illness. This is the last thing we want!

Make it a priority to ensure you are not holding on to any stagnant energy by using some energy-clearing techniques at the beginning and end of each day. Look at it like this: feeling miserable is energy's way of telling you to release something that is not serving you!

Exercise

Here is a wonderful technique to help shift unwanted negative energy.

When you are feeling overwhelmed with negativity, go and sit somewhere quiet for a few minutes, somewhere you know you'll not be disturbed, maybe your car, your bedroom, the dining room or, if you're at work, the toilet will do. I want you to sit down, close your eyes and take a few deep breaths. I want you to think of what is currently making you feel down: is it an argument you've had; is it stress from work overload; is it the kids being naughty; or perhaps money worries? What is it that's making you feel miserable?

Once you know, I want you to find the emotion behind that particular event or situation.

By 'emotion' I mean, how is the negative situation making you feel? Is it anger you're feeling; is it frustration, sadness, emptiness, melancholy, anxiety, worthlessness, loneliness, jealousy, resentment, blame, hatred, bitterness, apathy, boredom or concern? Find the emotion that you're currently feeling.

Don't get caught up in the drama of the situation that is causing the unwanted emotion; don't replay in your mind what is making you feel this way. Keep the drama out of your mind. All we're looking for here is the primary emotion.

Once you have found the emotion that is causing your unhappiness, take a deep breath and absorb yourself in feeling this emotion. For example, if you've had a really bad day, have had numerous arguments with your partner and you've outlined that the primary emotion you're experiencing is frustration, I want you to immerse yourself in the feeling of frustration.

It might sound like a complete contradiction to what we've been discussing so far, but bear with me.

Make sure you don't replay the arguments in your mind; that's not what we're looking for. Ensure you keep concentrating on feeling the frustration only. If your mind strays into the drama again, bring yourself back. Feel the feeling. Feel it!

Absorb your whole body in this feeling. Allow yourself to let it rise to the surface. It can do you no harm; it's just emotion. Stay with the sensation until you feel the intensity lift. This might take 10 seconds, it might take 30 seconds, it might take longer; just keep feeling the emotion until you feel it lift, or you find yourself getting bored. What you're doing is experiencing the emotion so you can release it. You're discharging any built-up or stagnant energy you've been retaining.

Once you've released the energy by doing this exercise, you'll find the frustration has disappeared. Gone! You'll have shifted any trapped energy that was causing you to feel the way you were. Remember, energy doesn't want to be trapped, it wants to move!

To recap:

- Find somewhere quiet and peaceful to sit or stand for a few minutes.

- Find out what's bothering you: your boss, the kids, the messy house?

- Uncover the primary emotion connected to what's bothering you.

- Absorb yourself in feeling just the emotion for a few minutes until you feel the energy shift.

- Take a deep breath and carry on with your day.

- Practise this exercise as many times as necessary throughout your day (normally once or twice is enough).

We've been taught, especially as children, that it's 'bad' to experience negative emotions. We shout at our children for getting angry, we try to hold back the tears when we're feeling upset, and the one about how 'real men don't cry' is a classic. As human beings we need to experience the whole array of emotions that we were born with. We need to let our children get angry and have tantrums if necessary; all they are really doing is releasing blocked negative energy, such as anger or frustration, and that's completely healthy. I'm not saying don't instil discipline; on the contrary, I am saying we should permit our children to learn to express their feelings in a safe way. Being taught to retain negative emotions is not healthy and it does us more harm in the long run; it can create all sorts of beliefs and odd behaviours in our adult lives. So if you're feeling angry, frustrated or sad, go and hit a pillow, scream out loud, have a good cry and let it all out. You know how good it feels when you cry? That's because you're releasing all your built-up negative energy!

It's important to point out, however, that once you've moved the unwanted energy, unless you consciously make an effort to change your thoughts thereafter, the frustration or whatever emotion you were experiencing will return. Once you've done the exercise on page 94, make sure you make every effort to stay in a positive frame of mind. Use your mood-shifter list, or whatever works for you, or you'll end up doing the exercise again and again.

I suggest you do this exercise only if you've tried everything else to lift your mood, including your mood-shifter list. If you don't release negative energy you will continue to experience the emotion and, through the Law of Attraction, your prolonged negative feelings will bring more of what you don't want into your life.

HOW TO MANIFEST YOUR DREAMS

OK, so now that you know the importance of being in tune with your feelings and how to change your mood and keep it on the up, how do you start to manifest your desired future or goals?

There are many techniques, and I can only speak from my experience and share the tried-and-tested ones that I have used for many years, and continue to use to this day.

Setting Your Goals

The first step in the process of manifesting your dreams is deciding what you actually want (i.e. *setting clear goals*). Now, this may sound simple, but if you are not absolutely clear about what you really want, the Law of Attraction cannot bring it to you. You will send out mixed vibrations and will therefore receive mixed results. Unfortunately this is what most of us have been doing all our lives.

> *Very few of us ever set ourselves measurable goals, and yet we then wonder why we are still doing the same thing, year in and year out. You need to take control.*

Remember, the universe is just picking up on your predominant thoughts and feelings, and replaying them back into your life. Your commands are not questioned: what you send out immediately begins to pull people, circumstances and events into your life that match your 'vibration frequency'.

You need to be very clear about what you want from your future. By becoming clear about your goals you are sending out clear and concise messages. The universe can then get to work on bringing your goals into your experience.

Believing and Trusting

This leads me on to the second step in the process of manifesting – belief and trust. Once we have a clear mental picture of the things we want, we need to trust that the universe has our request in hand. Our only job thereafter is to continue to keep our vibrations up, and not try to force things to happen. This is where many of us go wrong. The more we can continue to keep our vibrations up, the faster our goals will manifest in our lives without us having to make much effort at all.

For example, if you received a call from your mum and she announced that she had won a windfall on the Lottery and that she'd like to share some with you – you would start rejoicing immediately. You trust your mum implicitly; she's always kept her word and you know she will give you the money – you have no reason to doubt her. You don't wait until the money is in the bank before you start celebrating.

Another example: if you place your grocery order online, you know your request is being dealt with; you have no reason to think otherwise. You know it will arrive, so you relax.

These are two examples of the feeling you get when you know your goals will manifest. You need to start believing!

Once you have placed your 'order' with the universe, you need to trust that the universe will sort it out for you. You need to believe it's on its way, in exactly the same way you would trust your mum with the Lottery money or the supermarket with your grocery order. Don't worry, fret or think about your lack – you need to trust in the process.

You need to think, act, feel and speak as if your goal is on its way to you, as if it's inevitable.

Now, the universe isn't daft; we can't fool it (oh, how I wish we could). If you're continually thinking 'It hasn't arrived yet,' the message will be transmitted and you will continue to attract more 'lack'. If you believe you have your manifested goal already, the universe will move people, events and circumstance to bring them into your experience at record speed.

Believe You Have Achieved

OK, so how do you trust something without prior experience, and how do you start to believe you have achieved your goals already?

Trust is something earned over time but, as with everything, you have to start somewhere. So to ease you into the process, start by trying to manifest something small, like an extra £20 to buy yourself that scarf you saw last week, or how about manifesting a nice cup of tea or a big fat kiss? Start small. Build up trust in the process and then move on.

As for believing that your goals are already manifest, you need to start using your imagination! Do you remember being a child and playing make-believe? Yes? Well, this is what you need to start doing again. And of course it's been a while since we all did this, but it is tremendous fun! You could also try using affirmations or practising visualization.

Here are some techniques you can try to help you start believing:

- Vision board: go and buy a cork pinboard and start cutting out and collecting images or items you see in magazines or in your day-to-day life – pictures of your perfect man or house, or something that represents good health or love. Make your vision board colourful and happy, and put it somewhere prominent. Every time you look at it, it should invoke a warm and happy feeling.

- Role-play: have an imaginary conversation with yourself (the drive to work's a great opportunity to do this). Talk as if you were having a conversation with a friend, telling him or her about your success having now achieved your goals. What you're doing is jumping into the future and pretending your goal has already manifested. I love this one and do it all the time!

- Affirmations: as discussed earlier, do daily affirmations such as 'Money is flowing freely into my life' or 'My dream man is on his way to me right now.' Have fun with it!

- Visualization: spend 10 minutes a day dreaming about your future. Let nothing negative in, just dream about how your life will be once your goal has manifested in your life.

You could even try all four of these and manifest your goals at lightning speed!

Letting Go and Receiving

So we've talked about getting clear on what you want and how to start believing it is already yours. What comes next? Letting go and receiving.

This is where most people tend to give up or come unstuck. We decide what we want, we send that request off into the universe, we start to believe it's on its way, and then we get bored or disillusioned and end up going back to our old ways.

When we don't see instant results, we start trying to force things to happen, or try to work out exactly how they will happen, and in doing so we get in the way of the universe bringing them to us.

Allow the universe to do the work for you! While we are trying to work out how it will all happen, we are sending out a vibration of lack of faith, and hey, you've got it, the universe will simply bring us more lack of faith. It is just playing back what we are sending out. So, once we have decided what we want, it really is paramount that we let go and trust implicitly that it's on its way to us. You may struggle with this and find it almost impossible to 'let go'. You may send your 'order' out there and then 30 seconds later wonder why it hasn't arrived yet. You may find yourself trying to make things happen or forcing things into place. The result: it will simply slow things down. If you don't let the universe do its job, you will get in the way and sabotage your desires because you didn't trust that the universe would deliver them.

One of the biggest lessons in life is learning to let go. This has been a massive personal lesson for me. It has taken years for some of my goals to manifest, and quite often they never came about in the way I'd imagined. But I never lost hope! From time to time, when you feel fearful for whatever reason, you will fall into this old trap and start trying to control everything again. When you let go, amazing things start to happen, things you could have never dreamt of or created yourself. Over the years you will learn to have more trust that all will work out exactly as it should.

Once we have learned to let go, we need to become fully open to receiving. We need to keep our eyes and ears open for signs and hints that our goal is getting closer to us. We need to remember to tune in to our Inner Guide as much as possible. The more we continue to feel good and believe, the faster our goals will manifest. So what you're looking for are little signs in your day: it might be a brainwave that comes to you in the shower; it might be an email or a call, or something you find on the internet, or maybe someone you speak to. You need to remain open to the signs that the universe is giving you! Believe me, they are there.

It's important to point out that, although we live in a wonderful and magical world, we are still living in a physical reality and therefore we still need to take physical action. The difference, though, is that the action you decide to take will be action derived from your gut feeling or intuition, and not from your logical mind.

There is a huge difference. It's a bit like going for a walk on an extremely windy day. When you're walking with the wind coming towards you, you get buffeted and blown about. It feels uncomfortable and cold and it takes much longer to get where it is you want to go.

On the other hand, if you walk with the wind behind you, it carries you along and your journey is much more pleasant. The same applies to following your intuition. If it flows effortlessly, and feels good in the process, you know you're on track, but if it feels like you've got a hurricane in your face it may be time to consider turning around and going in the opposite direction. Feels good? You're on track. Feels bad? You're not.

Sometimes people get put off by the word 'action' as they think it implies hard work, but life shouldn't feel this way if you're heading in the right direction; it should feel effortless! Yes, some days will seem a little harder than others, but as a whole your journey should be a pleasant ride. I remember one particularly large goal I was working on a few years back; it wasn't until I'd achieved my goal that I became surprisingly aware of how effortless my journey had been from start to finish. It didn't feel like I'd taken much action at all, because it was so natural, easy and uncomplicated. I knew for sure that there was no way I could have figured out my path using just my logical mind alone. Nearly all the actions I'd taken had come from my gut or intuition. It really is amazing when everything just flows with minimal involvement from us!

If you can let go and be open to receiving, you will simply attract what you need to manifest what you desire.

> *If it's a certain website you need, you'll find it; if it's people you need, you will be attracted to them; if it's money you're short of, you'll attract it; if it's a new home, you'll find it; if it's a new*

job, you'll get it. You will attract everything you need in order to fulfil your dreams or desires. When the opportunity presents itself, when you get that impulse to do something or when you get that moment of clarity or insight, follow it! If it feels right, act. Don't delay; don't try to be too logical. Take one little step at a time and, before long, you will have reached your destination.

Everyone can do this; you don't have to be special, gifted, educated or rich – or, rather, you are already all of these things, you just didn't know it! We all have the ability to attract what we want. The only difference is that some of us choose to take responsibility for our lives and some of us don't realize that the choice is ours.

Now you have the knowledge, which option will you choose?

Remind yourself of how to manifest your goals:

- *Decide want you want. Set your goals. Get completely clear about what you desire from your future. Make sure it's something you really want and not something someone else wants you to do, have or be. It's time to get selfish.*

- *Let go. Don't try and figure it out or control the outcome.*

- *Trust and believe the universe is working behind the scenes to bring your order to you.*

- *Keep your vibrations up by feeling positive and grateful.*
- *Receive. Look out for all the signs and signals the universe presents to you.*
- *Take action. Make sure the action feels good – that way you know you're heading in the right direction.*

YOUR BELIEF SYSTEM AND THE LAW OF ATTRACTION

Once you start working with the Law of Attraction you will sometimes find that some things are easier to manifest than others. For example, you might find it really easy to manifest a parking space or a new outfit, yet trying to manifest more money into your life seems near impossible! Why? When you come up against this problem, you need to take a step back and look at your programming. By this I mean your limiting beliefs. Do you remember we talked in the previous chapter about how, once we have formed a belief, we will continue to live our lives by the rule of that particular belief, finding evidence along the way to support it? If you find the Law of Attraction isn't working in a particular area of your life, you need to look at what your underlying beliefs are about that area. If you are running a negative belief of some kind it will stop the universe from bringing your desire to fruition. It all starts with your beliefs. So if you come up against a roadblock, go back and do some of the exercises in Chapter 3. Answer the questions on page 52 again and set a plan of action to start changing your mindset. Once you change your beliefs, the universe can then deliver the goods. It's that's simple.

HOW LONG DOES MANIFESTING TAKE?

A lot of this will have to do with how many limiting beliefs you hold. The fewer you have, the easier it is to get the Law of Attraction to work for you. This is why I talk so extensively about your programming; this is where your journey must start. The more you believe in the Law of Attraction, the faster your manifestations will appear in your life.

Theoretically, if you think about it the universe doesn't see things as big or small. Everything is energy, therefore manifesting £1,000 should be no harder than manifesting £10; it is just our human collective belief that £1,000 must be harder to attract, simply because we deem it to be worth more. This is something we have been taught – it doesn't mean it is necessarily true. Again, it all boils down to a matter of belief. Do you believe it's harder to manifest £1,000 than £10? If you believe it, so be it. Expectation is a powerful thing. My advice to you is to start by trying to manifest small things, like £5 or a parking space. Once you can see the Law of Attraction working for you on a small scale, you can use your ability and newfound belief to move on to bigger things – manifesting your dream career, better health or a new home.

So how long do you think it will take: a week, a month, a year, ten years, or never? You decide. You will get what you expect. Period! This is why it's so important to become aware of your beliefs and how they are affecting your life.

According to Albert Einstein, time is just an illusion. What quantum physics tells us is that everything is happening simultaneously. It is we who think time is linear because we see things happening one after the other. We live our lives by the clock. Second after second, minute after minute and hour after hour. Try and be brave here, I know it's a mind-blowing concept, but if you understand that there is no time (well, not as we imagine) you will discover that our desired future already exists. It takes no time for the universe to manifest our goals; any perceived delay is simply caused by our belief about what is possible and what is not.

As you look at your current reality, remember not to feel bad or discouraged. Your current circumstances are simply a reflection of your beliefs and what you believe to be true. So if you're in debt you need to take a look at your personal beliefs around money and make sure you're actively working on new beliefs that will help you to attract and manifest money. It's the same with relationships. What is it you believe? Ask yourself how this might be affecting the relationships in your life. If you find you're not attracting what you want in life, it's time to stop and take a look at your mindset.

As you begin to work on your beliefs and to monitor your thoughts, using your feelings as a guideline, you will set the wheels in motion and you start to see results. It's like planting a seed in winter: you need to give it plenty of love and nurturing before you see the first shoots. So keep focused, have faith and, more than anything else, stay confident and positive about the process!

So there you have it. I told you it would get you thinking, didn't I? No one masters the art of manifesting overnight; it takes time, so don't be too hard on yourself. Remember, it has taken your whole lifetime to get to where you are now. I'm not saying it will take as long to change things, but you need to be patient. It's like unravelling a skein of wool: there'll be some detangling to do, but in the end it'll be worth it – I promise.

Exercise

Take each of the following areas and write down all the things you'd like to manifest within the next ten years. Have fun, dream... and write it down. Don't hold back, this is your life!

- *Travel* (e.g. visit the Italian Lakes or walk the Great Wall of China)

- *Skills and knowledge* (e.g. learn Spanish, try snowboarding or get a degree)

- *Experience* (e.g. ride a motorcycle or fly in a hot air balloon)

- *Career* (e.g. start a business, win a promotion or open a tea shop)

- *Finances* (e.g. pay off your credit cards, become debt free or pay your mortgage off early)

- *Relationships* (e.g. meet your perfect partner, get married or make amends with Mum)

- *Physical* (e.g. learn yoga or run a marathon)

YOUR HOMEPLAY THIS WEEK

- Read a book on the Law of Attraction or quantum physics.

- Start monitoring how you're feeling in any given moment: this is your barometer and will show you what you're attracting.

- Learn how to let go of negative emotions.

- Start your own daily gratitude journal.

- Make a list of all the things you'd like to manifest within the next ten years.

CHAPTER 5

Who You Really Are

Here we are at Chapter 5. I hope you're feeling invigorated, energized and not too bewildered. We've peeped inside the dark crevices of your mind to discover any limiting beliefs which may be lurking there, and have exposed how those beliefs may be sabotaging your success. We then delved a little deeper into your psyche to discover how to work with the universe to manifest your dreams. Now it is time for you to get to know yourself at a much deeper level. I mean really get to know yourself – all the things that make you *you*.

Are you ready to come face to face with yourself?

OK, so let's imagine you have cleared out all your old baggage – your limiting beliefs, childish habits and ridiculous behaviours – and you now feel squeaky-clean and shiny. What does that leave you with? Who are you now all those layers have been lifted off?

We have been running with our beliefs, habits and behaviours since the day we were able to open our eyes, and we lost touch with our blueprint, or authentic self, long, long ago. In fact, we are so convinced of our beliefs, habits and behaviours that, once we start to change the patterns we've been clinging to all our lives, it may feel as if we have lost the use of a limb.

Suppose this feeling is a fear of the unknown: 'If I don't play the superhero, what on Earth will I do with my time? Who will I become?' When you embark on a journey of self-discovery you are committing to change, and in the process letting go of anything that no longer serves you. But in doing so, you determine a new path, a new future and, ultimately, a new you. You need to let go of the old to receive the new. And, believe me, the new you is *far better* than you can possibly imagine. It's a bit like my wardrobe: so crammed with clothes that I no longer wear that I simply can't squeeze any more in. The clothes overflow and my husband starts to moan about what a mess the bedroom looks. When it gets to this point it's time to de-clutter and throw out the items that are no longer needed – which, of course, just makes room for some new clothes! It's the same with your life. Letting go leaves room for new events, situations and people to enter your life. Holding on to someone or something is never any good for us; in fact, it's very damaging because we stop ourselves from receiving more good things. Remember, energy wants to move!

HOW DO I GET TO KNOW MYSELF?

You need to rediscover your unique blueprint, which holds within it your personality, talents, passions and the values that make you who you are. There are people who have a natural talent for making people laugh, for healing or for Nature. As noted earlier, there are also those who have a natural talent for creating inspiring works of art, for playing a musical instrument or for singing in tune without effort. It's this differentiation that makes the world such a wonderful place in which to live. And we *all* have passions, values and talents. If your Inner Critic is telling you otherwise, tell him or her (politely!) to shut up until you've finished this section of the book.

> *Each one of us shares the common purpose of contributing something of value to this world by using our unique set of passions, values and talents.*

Unfortunately, as also mentioned before, our blueprint gets covered up early on in life when our parents, teachers or friends tell us, 'You'll never be able to do that,' 'You're just not clever enough' or 'You can't do that, it's far too expensive.' We accept these restrictions as the limitations of our world and our lives. We drift off-course and then we wonder how on Earth we came to be in the situation we're in. Our beliefs take over our lives and direct us to destinations we would never have dreamed of visiting. A strong indication that you are living your life by someone else's rules or beliefs is that you can't make decisions for yourself; you don't trust your gut feelings and instead seek out 'expert' advice; you hate shopping for a new outfit because you haven't got a clue what suits you; you end up going along with everyone else's ideas instead of your own and then come to resent it.

When we follow our unique blueprint it will bring us increased joy and happiness. This blueprint is the fundamental bedrock of who we are. So if we know what our blueprint is, we can start to build a life around it, thereby increasing our overall happiness and joy. It's only when our lives are in conflict with our blueprint that we become discontented and unhappy.

In general, if an area in your life isn't working (such as a job or relationship), it's off-balance with your blueprint and this may be an opportunity for you to re-assess it. For example, I could easily have become a maths teacher (at a very basic level), but maths was not a subject I enjoyed, nor was I particularly good at it, so to base a career on it would have been futile. Instead, I decided to create a career I truly enjoyed, which encompassed all my natural skills, strengths and abilities. The result: I love what I do and wake up each morning with a spring in my step and passion for the day ahead.

When you uncover your blueprint, things fall into place naturally and you suddenly feel like you're not swimming against the tide any more. Things flow smoothly, they fall into place effortlessly and life becomes a joy to live!

Think back to the windy day scenario mentioned earlier: if you feel like you've got a hurricane blowing in your face, it's the universe's way of saying 'You're going the wrong way, turn around!'

I want to share with you how to set about uncovering your own unique blueprint. First off, we're going to take a look at your values.

Are you ready?

UNCOVERING YOUR VALUES

The first step to uncovering your values is to find out what it is in life that brings you joy. Once you have figured out what brings you joy, you'll have a clearer picture of the make-up of your blueprint.

Now when I say 'joy', I'm talking about those moments in your life, big or small, when you feel sheer pleasure or bliss (you can't include sex in this exercise – sorry!). Moments when your heart swells with joy, your body bubbles over with love, when you feel totally at peace with yourself or the world, or when you feel exhilarated about something. It's that moment when you think, 'I'm really happy.'

Your Inner Critic may choose this moment to pop up and inform you that you can't recall any moments of joy or happiness recently. Rubbish, of course you can! If you're struggling to think of instances, you're thinking too hard. A simple 'Thank you' from someone that you opened a door for may be a moment of bliss or peace. We all know that being thanked is a wonderful feeling and can really brighten up our day.

In a minute I'm going to ask you to write in your journal or on a blank piece of paper six experiences that have brought you joy or happiness within the last two years.

To help you along, here is a list of my own six experiences. As you will see, most of these experiences are actually quite small. They're simple pleasures.

1. Sitting by the river on a sunny day with my husband and kids, eating ice-cream.

2. Creating balance within my day for all my earthly duties, spending quality time with my family and finding time for 'me' and my own personal development.

3. Waking up on a Sunday morning and not having to do anything I don't want to do! (Rare, but great when it happens.)

4. Being thanked, whether that's at work, by a friend or in the street!

5. Reading a wonderful new book.

6. Writing an inspirational article.

Exercise

Now write down your own six experiences. You really need to take some time to think about this; it's important to reflect on all the things, big and small, that have given you that wonderful warm feeling of pleasure or bliss inside. Go and make yourself a nice cup of tea and spend some time reminiscing. Go on, do it now!

Experience 1 _____
_____

Experience 2 _____
_____

Experience 3 _____
_____

Experience 4 _____
_____

Experience 5 _____
_____

Experience 6 _____
_____

Once you have your list of six experiences, you need to work out what the underlying value is in each experience. It's very simple: ask yourself what each of your experiences gave you? What value did you, or do you, get from each one?

To give you an idea of what I mean, let me share with you the underlying value of my six experiences:

1. Sitting by the river on a sunny day with my husband and kids, eating ice-cream = Love and security

2. Creating balance within my day for all my earthly duties, spending quality time with my family and finding time for 'me' and my own personal development = Harmony

3. Waking up on a Sunday morning and not having to do anything I don't want to do (rare, but great when it happens!) = Freedom

4. Being thanked, whether that's at work, by a friend or in the street! = Appreciation

5. Reading a wonderful new book = Inspiration or learning new things

6. Writing an inspirational article = Achievement

I now know that my values are:

1. Love and security
2. Harmony
3. Freedom
4. Appreciation
5. Inspiration and learning new things
6. Achievement.

And it's not just the scenarios outlined above that can give me the experience of those particular values. For example, achievement may be met in many different ways, not just by writing an article. It could be baking a cake, running a workshop or even decorating the bedroom. It really doesn't matter what you do to meet your values, as long as they are met. The more your values are met, the happier you'll be.

Exercise

Now, write down what your own six values are. Here are some key words to help you along:

freedom, nature, harmony, appreciation, love, learning, fun, achievement, excitement, balance, variety, advancement, security, peace, loyalty, creativity, friendship, stability, power, variety, spirituality, adventure, affection, openness, excellence, justice, abundance, integrity, making a difference, routine, protection, adventure, originality, wisdom, education, discipline, playfulness, respect, serenity, honesty.

Value 1 _____

Value 2 _____

Value 3 _____

Value 4 _____

Value 5 _____

Value 6 _____

Now you have worked out your six values, answer the following questions.

- *What areas of my life are currently in conflict with my values? For example, not enough 'me' time or being in a job where no one ever says, 'Thank you'.*

- *What needs to happen in order to change this?*

- *What small step can I make this week to start working towards this change?*

This week, make it your intention to meet as many of your values as possible. Make a plan of action to do more of the things you enjoy and see what difference it makes to your overall wellbeing at the end of the week.

YOUR TALENTS, SKILLS AND STRENGTHS

Alongside our values sit our natural talents, skills and strengths: things that we enjoy doing and which come easily to us. Our natural talents often start to emerge in early childhood. When we are children we all instinctively know what we enjoy doing, what comes naturally and what we're good at. It may be building sandcastles or playing with toy bricks, drawing pictures, dancing or singing, reading, doing puzzles, etc.

It's quite interesting to watch children at play and notice the things that they are naturally drawn to doing in their free time. Some children just love the fresh air and at the first opportunity dart outside to play; some are naturally arty and are always keen to show you their latest picture; others are often to be found in a corner reading their favourite book; others are making music from an early age (even if that means banging on pots and pans!).

Unfortunately, as we get older we lose touch with our own natural abilities. Our talents tend to get covered up quite early on in life and many of us have lost touch with them by the time we reach our early twenties. We forget who we are. Many of my clients seem to have lost their way. They've spent 20 years doing an unfulfilling job and have no idea how they actually got there. It happens to so many of us. We fall into a job or career and we plod along for years, forgetting about our values and talents, passions, forgetting about who we really are and what makes us tick. But then, years later, we find ourselves lost and without direction. We spend so many years following the crowd that we find ourselves far from home with no idea how to get back.

Well, it's time to reclaim your youth, to remember who you were when you were dancing around the living room performing for your aunties and uncles, or when you came in at the end of the day with mud up to your armpits after looking for creepy-crawlies. I want to encourage you to bring those feelings back and remember your childhood as best you can. I appreciate it may seem like many moons ago, so how about digging out some old photos to evoke some memories, or maybe talking to your family about their recollections to discover what you left behind?

If you can't remember the exact thing you liked doing, just find a substitute. What was it that you enjoyed most about performing in front of your aunties and uncles or getting your hands dirty? Was it entertaining others? Being the centre of attention? Enjoying Nature? Learning about the world?

Exercise

To help you to uncover your natural talents, answer the following questions. Remember to be as specific as possible and think back over your entire life and, most importantly, write everything down, no matter how silly it appears to be – don't edit yourself!

- *When growing up, what did people say you were gifted at or had a talent for?*

- *What do you find comes easily to you?*

- *What makes you excited, animated and lights up your face?*

- *What enjoyable experience makes you lose all sense of time?*

- *What are you drawn to doing?*

- *What would you gladly spend your money on to be able to do?*

- *What activities would you do if money were not an issue?*

- *What things do you pick up faster than others?*

- *What do you do that amazes others?*

- *If you were to ask your family or friends what your natural talents are, what would they say?*

Now write down what insights you've had from doing this exercise. For example, 'I used to love swimming but I haven't swum in the last 15 years' or 'I used to enjoy doing arts and crafts at school, yet I now spend all my time working in an office doing admin.'

If you could define four of your natural talents, what would they be? (For example, 'people person', 'creative hands', 'great singing voice', 'fantastic cook', 'good listener'.) If you get stuck listing your four talents, ask your friends, family or partner for help.

Here are some example talents, skills and strengths to get you thinking: singing, entertaining, nurturing, making people laugh, being optimistic, leadership, teamwork, learning, investigating, helping, debating, campaigning, experimenting, de-cluttering, teaching, writing, painting, playing, analysing, motivating, advising, networking, meditating, communicating, coaching, public speaking, sports.

Exercise

List your top four natural talents:

Talent 1 _____

Talent 2 _____

Talent 3 _____

Talent 4 _____

Now answer the following questions.

- *Is there one special talent, skill or strength that stands out above the others?*

- *As a percentage, how much of your talent, skill or strength are you using in your everyday life?*

- *How can you start using your talents, skills or strengths more?*

- *If you were to make a living using your talents, skills or strengths, what would you do?*

This week, make it your intention to use as many of your talents, skills or strengths as possible. Make a plan of action to do more of the things you enjoy and see what a difference it makes to your overall well-being at the end of the week.

WHAT ACTIVITIES DO YOU LOVE TO DO?

Take a look at the list below and think about times in your life when you've felt really happy, connected, passionate, excited, confident and fulfilled because of something you've been doing. Think of both current things and things from the past.

Here are some examples to get you thinking: talking, writing, painting, performing, teaching, designing, sewing, building using your hands, arts and crafts, acting, singing, entertaining, photographing, inspiring, empowering, healing, making a difference, creating, cooking, dancing, exercising, meditating, tasting, eating, travelling, interviewing, mentoring, organizing, fishing, fundraising, planning, initiating projects, composing music, negotiating, gardening, sailing, skiing, diving, sports, chatting, designing, debating, campaigning, experimenting, laughing, joking, making people laugh, writing, de-cluttering.

If something isn't listed, just add it!

Exercise

What five activities have you always enjoyed the most?

1 _____

2 _____

3 _____

4 _____

5 _____

- *What it is about this activity you love so much?*
- *Is there something new you'd like to try?*
- *Is there something you used to do but haven't in recent years for whatever reason?*
- *If you could earn money doing an activity you enjoy, what would it be?*

WHAT MAKES YOU TICK AND WHY?

I have another little exercise for you to try which will help you to understand what things you're naturally drawn to and why. I want you to list your top five favourite things in each of the following categories. Say why they are your favourites; describe how you feel when you think about or experience these favourite things, and think about how you can inject more of these into your life.

Exercise

List your top five favourite:

- *films*

- *shops*

- *songs*

- *books*

- *quotes*

- *foods*

- *activities or interests*

- *places to visit*

- *cultures.*

What is the common theme coming through? What have you learned about yourself?

Now that you are starting to become aware of your blueprint, you are closer to uncovering your true self. Most people travel throughout life without really knowing who they are or what drives them. So now you know you need to start building your life around you. Start making small changes immediately. The more you can live your life in line with your unique blueprint, the happier, more fulfilled and confident you will become. And that's a promise!

YOUR LIFE PURPOSE

'Life purpose' is an interesting topic. Do I think we all have a predetermined purpose that we must discover in order to find fulfilment and happiness? No! Sorry if that's not the answer you're looking for, but I believe our purpose here on Earth is what we make it. Our true purpose is to add value to the world in some way and to be happy in the process. Living a life utilizing our talents and skills and fulfilling our values and interests will ultimately bring us the happiness we are all subconsciously searching for. We must stop looking for career nirvana – there isn't one thing out there, there are many options, so many things you can enjoy if you open your eyes.

When I first discovered my own blueprint, I quickly realized that the job I was doing didn't really fit with what I wanted from a career any more. In fact, it helped me make more sense of why I had become so miserable. One of my most important values is appreciation. I like to feel appreciated; I like to be thanked and valued. The company I was working for at the time had recently been through a buy-out and, while nothing had changed in terms of the day-to-day running of the business, the management team had been replaced. Six months into the takeover, the cracks were starting to show and people were leaving in droves. I had gone from being well-respected and appreciated by the previous management to being viewed as just part of the furniture: the new managers had no understanding of my role or what motivated me. Over time my enthusiasm diminished and I became apathetic and uninterested. My values weren't being met any more. And while I wasn't consciously aware of this at the time, subconsciously I knew something was amiss. I wasn't happy.

Having awareness and a clear definition of my values and talents, skills and strengths, interests and passions helped me to readjust and point my career back in the direction I wanted it to go. Now, this readjusting didn't happen overnight. It was a process which took time, but without this awareness the process probably wouldn't have been so smooth, and perhaps would have taken far longer than it did. The great thing about understanding your blueprint is you can use it as a guide to where you currently are, and where it is you want to go.

Exercise

Write down your values, talents and interests on a piece of paper and put it somewhere you can see it every day – as a reminder to live your life 'on purpose'. Keep your eyes and ears open to new opportunities and, when something arises, a new idea or something someone says that strikes a chord with you, take action and follow your inner guidance. Make it your job from now on to live your life in alignment with your blueprint, and see what remarkable changes accrue.

FINDING YOUR IDEAL CAREER

There are many people in the UK today who dislike their job or chosen profession. A recent survey showed that people in the UK are unhappier than those in any other Western nation. I wonder why? As mentioned, many of us fall into a particular job or career without giving our values, passions and talents a second thought. But how can you build a suitable career without knowing your blueprint? The truth is, you can't.

It wasn't until I uncovered mine that I suddenly realized I was in the wrong profession. It came as a bit of a shock when I discovered that I hardly used any of my talents, skills or strengths, and that very few of my values were being met, but having a greater understanding of what made me tick helped me to see clearly which careers were right for me and which weren't. I then had the clarity to point my working life in the right direction.

Before this chapter draws to a close, I want you to take a look at your current line of work and evaluate if you are in the right job for you. If not, investigate what would be right for you.

Did you know that an average working week is 48 hours long – and far longer for many people?

Many of us spend more time at work than we do at home with our families, so it has never been more important to ensure that we enjoy our work. Working shouldn't just be about earning enough to pay the bills, put food on the table or buy the necessities of life. Of course all these things are essential, but your working life should be fulfilling, rewarding and enriching as well. Having a job that provides all of these things nurtures the soul. There is nothing more gratifying than feeling you are making a contribution to the world, whether that's by working on a supermarket check-out, in an office or volunteering to work with the sick and infirm.

> *On this planet we should all help others by utilizing and sharing our unique talents.*

So let me ask you an important question: do you enjoy your line of work?

Be honest with yourself. Just because your job pays well, provides flexi-time, gives you 30 days' holiday, a good pension, health insurance, a company car and an easy commute, does not mean that it is fulfilling, rewarding and enriching. You're fooling yourself; it just means you're comfortable and probably too scared even to dare to consider making a move for fear of losing these privileges. If you're in the right job you should wake up in the morning with a spring in your step knowing that today you're going to make a difference to the world and add value in some way.

So let me ask you: do you *really* enjoy your job?

Exercise

Answer the following seven questions.

1. *Which of my talents are currently being used in my job?*

2. *Which values are being met in my current job?*

3. *What three things do I hate about my job?*

4. *What three things do I love about my job?*

5. *How do I feel about going to work every day?*

6. *What three things would I love to change about my job if I could?*

7. *On a scale of 1 to 10, how good is my work-life balance at the moment?*

By answering these questions you should be starting to get a clearer picture of whether you're in the right profession or not.

Just because you may have revealed that your job isn't providing you with the fulfilment your soul is yearning for, this does not always mean you have to run out and find a new occupation or retrain to do something else. It's not as clear-cut as that. For some, a total career change is absolutely the right thing to do, but for others it's just a case of making a few small changes, such as re-addressing your working hours, working from home one day a week, having a pay increase, moving desks or relocating to another office closer to home. Small changes can make a world of difference. So look again at your answers to the above questions. Is it just a few small changes that are required, or is it total career shift?

One of my clients was worried that she was in the wrong profession. She was scared that she'd spent eight years training only to find out it wasn't the career for her, and she was terrified of what her family and friends would think if she gave it all up. When we started looking at her values and talents it became apparent that it wasn't the actual job itself that was the problem; her work–life balance was throwing her off-kilter. All that was required was to make some small changes to her working day. We decided that because she was constantly watching the clock, stressing herself unnecessarily, she would leave her wristwatch at home and remove the clock from her office wall. We also decided that instead of working through her lunch break, which she did every day, she would ensure she took a break at least three times a week. She also started walking to work and took up some other activities in the evenings. When I spoke to my client two weeks later the change was phenomenal: she was a much brighter, happier and more contented person. That's all it took!

But for those of you who know deep down that no matter how many changes you make to your job it will never be right for you, it's time to get clear about what you *do* want to do.

BUT I DON'T KNOW WHAT I WANT TO DO!

Career changes are probably one of the most common topics I'm faced with as a life-coach. Clients tell me they're unhappy doing what they're doing, but have no idea what they want to do instead.

Deep down, if we're completely honest with ourselves, we all have ideas about what we'd love to do, but we're too scared to admit it, or think we're too old, or that it's simply unfeasible for whatever reason. We often dismiss our ideas as silly and outlandish, and most of us take these ideas to our deathbed without ever acting upon them.

You don't have to endure a job that bores you to tears! You don't have to waste your life doing unfulfilling work. There are thousands and thousands of career options out there if we look hard enough. You only have to look at your immediate circle of family and friends to see this.

I'd like to share with you my six-step plan to making your own personal career shift.

1. Build Your Career Blueprint

Before you start scouring the internet in search of a better job, it's vital that you create your career blueprint, as this will help you to know which jobs you'll be best suited to. Once you can get clear about your blueprint you can then be more objective about your future career decisions. Get a blank piece of paper and create six columns.

1. List all of your interests and passions – animals, books or cars.

2. List your skills, talents and abilities – good listener, problem-solver, bargain-hunter!

3. List all your job likes and dislikes – working solo, working in a team or having a dictatorial boss.

4. List your favourite types of working environment – outside, in a large team, travelling around.

5. List your boundaries and benefits – want to earn *X* per year, have a company car or health care.

6. List your ideal working location – from home, within a 6-mile radius or in a large city/town.

2. Get Your Ideas Down

Now you have done the important part of under-standing yourself and building your career blueprint, it's time to get your thinking cap on and start exploring your options. DO NOT hold back! Let go of ANY limiting thinking and just let your ideas flow, both the logical and pie-in-the-sky. When you've finished, ask yourself which three ideas are really jumping off the page? Which three ideas really excite you and why?

3. Do Your Homework

OK, so you've got your ideas down on paper – what now? It's time to start exploring each of your options.

Do not close the door until you've fully explored each one. Find out as much as you can about each type of work. The best way to find out what a job is really like is to get some hands-on experience. Go and volunteer, get your hands dirty and see how this influences your decisions. Most importantly, use your career blueprint to establish whether this path is *really* right for you.

4. Create Your Vision

Career transitions can be scary. I know: I've been there! What's important is to create a vision of your future life. Get a piece of paper and imagine that 6–12 months have passed and you're now doing something you truly love. What would your day look like, what would be happening and how would you be feeling? Write down as much detail as you can and then stick your vision on your wall as a reminder of where you're heading. Remember: all successful people see their success long before it actually happens. Create *your* vision now and get clear about what you want!

5. Time to Get into Action

It's all very well getting clear about your blueprint and researching your ideas, but without physical action, nothing will really change. It's time to create your plan of action. Think about all the milestones you're going to have to tackle during your transition to your new career, from funding, training, research and so on. Break your goal down into smaller milestones so you don't get too overwhelmed. Your aim is to then take just five action steps each week.

6. Get Support

Making any life-change can be tough, so it's important you create your 'tribe' – a team of people who can support and help you along the way. List all the people in your life whom you believe can assist you on your journey: family, friends, neighbours, old workmates. You'll be surprised at just how large your network is and just how many different skills you can pull upon if needed.

This is exactly what I did when I first discovered life-coaching. I knew nothing about the industry other than I thought it sounded fascinating. I had no idea what training was needed or how much it would cost me. And I had absolutely no idea how to start up and run a successful business. Yet here I am years later, running my own company. I've found a career that truly inspires me, combines all my interests, my skills, talents and values but, more importantly, I've found something I'm truly passionate about in life – helping others to achieve their full potential!

Once you find a career in line with your blueprint, life has a way of just flowing; all of a sudden it feels like we're not fighting any more, and everything just falls into place. We all deserve to do work we truly love!

We're all looking for a fairy godmother to sort everything out for us. But life doesn't work this way. We have to instigate the magic, so don't be put off if your ideal career means retraining or learning new skills. If it's right for you, you'll find a way. There might be some temporary hard work, but it's only transitory, it will soon pass. You can make as many excuses as you want, but the buck stops with you. Don't waste your life doing unfulfilling work; share your wonderfulness with the world!

YOUR HOMEPLAY THIS WEEK

1. Make a list of your values and put them up somewhere you'll see them daily.

2. Start living your blueprint, getting your values met as often as you can, doing activities that you're passionate about, using your natural talents, skills and strengths in whatever way you can.

3. Define your career blueprint and work out if your current job is right for you.

4. Brainstorm all the jobs or careers you'd love to have, and start to research their viability.

CHAPTER 6

Beyond Your Physical Self

Let me now share with you a very personal experience I had a few years ago which opened my eyes to a whole new way of living. This 'new way' has led me to become a life-coach and inspired me to write this book.

Let me tell you about the day that changed my life forever.

It was a freezing cold, bitter January afternoon. I had finished work and was driving to pick my daughter up from nursery. I pulled up outside, parking in my normal space by the railings, next to a large oak tree. I could see the sun setting in the distance and noticed two tiny robins in the tree hopping from branch to branch with no regard for my close proximity. I was 20 minutes early and under any other circumstances I would have gone straight into the nursery to collect my daughter, but I held back and took the opportunity to read a few pages of a book I had been given by a friend. This book had captivated me and I was tremendously excited by its content, as somewhere deep inside me I felt a resonance I hadn't felt before.

As I sat there with the car engine running and the windscreen slowly misting up, I turned the pages and found myself reading a meditation. In those days meditation was unfamiliar territory to me, and my uneducated assumptions about meditation consisted of rather unpleasant-smelling josh sticks and old men sitting cross-legged humming mantras. But, despite my limited understanding, I decided to take the opportunity to give it a go. I remember reading this little meditation two or three times, it was very simple; in fact, it was so simple I didn't quite see the point. Anyway, after making sure I had memorized the words, I inhaled deeply, closed my eyes and in my head repeated the words I had memorized.

I don't think there are enough words in the English dictionary to describe what happened next.

As I sat in my car on that very normal January afternoon, something huge happened – not externally, but something happened inside me that was to change my world forever. As I effortlessly and with no expectations repeated the words of this short meditation in my head, all of a sudden an almighty gush of what I can only describe as 'energy' entered my chest, moved up through the top half of my body and left out of the top of my head. This energy was unearthly; it was not something that I had experienced before and it was a more powerful feeling than anything I had felt in my entire life. This energy felt like total love, or euphoria. It was all-consuming and overwhelming. It's hard to say how long it lasted, but it was probably only 10 or 15 seconds. But in those few seconds my life changed. What the hell was it? My mind was racing and the tears were rolling down my face. I threw the book to the floor in shock. I couldn't make sense of the experience; there was no logical or rational explanation for it. It was very difficult for me to take in, as I've always been a fan of hard facts and figures to back things up – I've never been the airy-fairy type. The only thing I could think of was to call my grandmother, who was a practising Christian. After spending 40 minutes on the telephone I felt calmer, and composed myself enough to go into the nursery to collect my daughter (by this time I was almost an hour late!).

In those remarkable few seconds I knew with all certainty that there was far more to life than I had been led to believe. I had discovered my inner spirit. My journey of awakening had begun! In those few moments I had moved beyond my physical body, beyond my mind to touch the world of spirit or pure energy, pure love and fulfilment itself. I had touched the 'real me'. My comfortable reality had been turned upside-down and it took a few days before I felt 'with it', so to speak.

My journey still continues, but I can tell you one thing: since that moment of realization my life has flourished, grown, expanded and, for the first time, has far more meaning than I ever thought possible.

It's important to point out that just because I had such a so-called 'spiritual' experience, it didn't mean that from that point onwards my life was all rosy. What has happened, though, is that since that time my life has made more sense and became far richer as a result.

I spent a long time trying to process and understand what happened to me that day. I read book after book, from religious books to books on quantum physics. I talked to mentors and spiritual gurus who I hoped could help me to understand and assimilate my experience. After a long search, I am happy to say I have come to a comfortable resting place.

> My conclusion is this: *beyond the physical body, with all its imperfections and ailments, and far beyond the brain with its duff programming, we are spiritual (or energy) beings living in a physical reality. We are here as spiritual beings to play the game of life.*

We are conditioned to our material existence; we take life at face value and are accustomed to using only our five senses – sight, smell, touch, taste and hearing. Spirit is beyond all of these. It lies beneath the radar of our physical awareness, and this is why so few people find it in their lifetime.

Spirit, or energy, is all there is and it's the 'real you' not the 'you' you have been fooled into believing you are. Spirit is pure fulfilment and love, and the more we connect with our inner spirit, the more fulfilling and satisfying our lives become.

Our bodies are our costume and our brains are our computer processor. But our brains, with their limiting thinking, and our bodies, with their imperfections and illnesses, aren't what make us who we really are. The real you is pure positive energy – pure fulfilment itself!

Energy cannot die or be extinguished; it just changes form. This, in turn, means that we never die; we just change our form. Our time on Earth is not the end of the story; we are forever ongoing. We are here to enjoy our time on Earth: to live, to play, to love, to experience all that this wonderful planet has to offer. Unfortunately, our lack of awareness means that our limited understanding covers up and distorts this vital truth.

> But here is the key that I have come to learn: the more we connect with our inner spirit, the more pleasurable, smooth and gratifying our ride through this life becomes, and the less we have to control, push, use force and manipulate things into being. Spirit has the ability to do this for us, if we allow it.

This is a spiritual universe, from start to finish. This is the secret that we've all been missing. The more we can connect to our inner spirit, the more harmonious our lives will become. Simple! There is a revolution afoot. People and science are starting to wake up to this truth. When we really get a grasp of this, life is never really the same again. We must see through the mind's bravado to the truth. It is the collective mind (world beliefs) that has led us astray, and we just need to raise our consciousness to see through this illusion.

Our inner spirit has the ability to re-programme our minds for us, if we let it.

So what does all this mean? It means we are not limited, small, inadequate or restricted in any way, as previously thought. We can be, do or have whatever we desire with help from our inner spirit. We just need to realize it and start believing! When we do, our lives will change dramatically forever, and so will our entire human existence.

Once you learn how to connect to your inner spirit, people, circumstances, events, situations and opportunities will appear seemingly out of thin air to fulfil your every need. As if by magic! We can all connect with our inner power. We all have the ability to do this, but most of us don't know that this extraordinary power exists right at our fingertips. It's waiting there for us to wake up to so it can start helping us to manifest the life we deserve: a life full of bliss, harmony, peace, love and abundance.

In a moment I'm going to show you how you can start connecting with your own inner spirit.

I have told you this story because I want you to open your mind to new possibilities, not so that you can try and re-create such an experience for yourself (spiritual awakening happens to each person in a different way). I want you to expand your awareness beyond your physical existence. I urge you to seek your own answers. Do not take my word for it, or anyone else's for that matter. Your own truth lies with you, right now. To follow someone else's path is futile. The best strategy is to discover your own truth. Others may inspire, guide, give you direction, but ultimately you have to cut your own way through the jungle. Some people will tell you to head north, others will tell you to head south, and both will believe their way is right (and, of course, it is for them), but you alone can find your own true north or south.

FEAR OF THE UNKNOWN

I know all this talk about energy or your inner spirit may be a little hard to digest, but no one's asking you to change your beliefs overnight. Self-discovery is an ongoing journey. In fact, does it ever end? Once we discover one thing, something else crops up and surprises us. But growth is our key to freedom. The more we learn, understand and experience, the more free we become, and it's a wonderful process. Take your time; there is no rush!

Just remember, everyone feels fear on his or her journey to a better life. I've yet to meet the person who hasn't. Fear is a normal part of the growth process, whether it is fear about achieving a particular goal or fear of growing spiritually. Fear is a common part of everyday life, and the sooner people realize this, the sooner they will stop running away and allow themselves to grow.

THE JOY OF GOING WITHIN

After my profound experience in the car that January day, I decided that in order to find the answers I was looking for I needed to learn more about spirituality and my own inner spirit. I decided that my first port of call would be meditation. I downloaded articles from the internet on how to meditate. I bought books and CDs and, eventually, after trying lots of different techniques, I found my own style, my own way, which I still use to this day. How has this affected my life? Well, the results have been profound. I revealed a tranquillity that I'd never experienced before. I found an almighty support within that I didn't even know existed, and I found a clarity to my thinking which enabled me to see beyond all the limiting beliefs and behaviours that I'd been holding on to since I was a child. In short, meditating changed my entire world and helped me shape the life I am living today.

I believe if more people were to understand the benefits of meditation and make it part of their daily routine we would live in a far more harmonious world. Modern life is manic; we have been fooled into living our lives using our minds as our confidants. But our minds are programmed with all sorts of limiting beliefs which invariably wreak havoc in our lives. We need to bypass our minds as much as possible and connect directly with our inner spirit; that way our lives will be far more peaceful and enjoyable.

Most of us live our lives by the clock, and at speed: we go to bed late, we get up before the sun has even risen and we pollute our bodies with unhealthy toxins. When we allow ourselves to 'go within', using meditation as a tool, time slows down, we clear our minds of negative clutter, we become less stressed and, more importantly, we feel happier. Plus it's free and accessible to everyone – yet many people spend millions of pounds each year buying drugs which they think will make them feel more vibrant, or indulge in material pleasures which they believe will bring them contentment. It's crazy when the solution is so simple.

I'd like to introduce you to three methods of going within and connecting with your own inner spirit. First, I want to show you how to meditate; second, I'd like to explain how positive visualization can change your life for the better and help you to achieve your goals; lastly, I'd like to talk to you about the power of prayer.

MEDITATION

There are numerous styles of meditating, such as breathing, focusing on a candle, walking or using mantras, and there are lots of different schools of meditation such as Buddhist, tantric and transcendental, to name but three. You have to find what works for you.

The technique below is my own personal style; it is what I find works best for me, given my own schedule and routine. But before I share my chosen method with you, I'd like you to consider the following tips:

- *Create your sanctuary*. Where is the best place for you to relax and where you're not likely to be disturbed? Perhaps the spare room, the garden, the dining room or even in the bath? Decide on the most suitable place and stick to the same location each time you meditate.

- *Use whatever you have to help you relax*. Consider lighting a candle while you meditate, or having a special ornament, photo or vase of flowers next to you. Anything that will help you to feel more at ease and relaxed.

- *Decide on your posture while meditating.* There are many different postures, from the most commonly known Lotus position to the Egyptian, half-lotus, quarter-lotus and Japanese. You need to do a little research and see which one you prefer. I just lie down on my bed with my legs uncrossed and hands by my side, as I find this most relaxing.

- *Don't be disturbed.* Switch off the phone, lock the door and ensure you're not likely to be interrupted. You might meditate in the evenings when the kids are in bed and you can be reasonably certain you're not going to be disturbed.

- *Write down any insights or thoughts.* Consider keeping a journal of your experiences or any insights that may crop up while you're meditating. When you become more proficient at meditating you'll start noticing you get more ideas during meditation or immediately afterwards.

- *Don't be scared.* If you feel anxious or uncomfortable for any reason while meditating, remember you are not going anywhere so there is no need for fear. Meditating is not a form of 'medium-ship'. All you are doing is quieting your mind. You are going inwards in search of self-awareness. If you do begin to feel fearful, just open your eyes slowly and bring your focus back to your surroundings.

- *Be guided by a voice.* While learning to meditate you may find it useful to record your own voice to use as a guided meditation, or perhaps you might like to consider buying a guided meditation CD to follow until you feel comfortable doing it on your own.

- *Commit.* You must find time to integrate this new routine into your daily schedule, just like brushing your teeth or taking a shower. If you're inconsistent, the results you receive will be inconsistent, so make a commitment to meditate as regularly as you can.

Start off with just 5 minutes' meditation a day, building up to 30 minutes or longer. Or try small 3-minute meditations throughout your day. Sometimes life may be very busy, but the more you meditate the more you'll start noticing the positive effects it has on you. You'll probably find your mind will be extremely active at first, reminding you of all the things you need to do, like the laundry, phoning your sister, making the kids' lunches for the next day, and so on. This is normal; you need to persist and eventually the nagging voices will fade away and you'll be left with the most wonderful feeling of peace and bliss.

Below I have outlined three simple meditations for you to try.

Relaxation

Take up your chosen position, close your eyes, relax and start noticing your breathing – breathe in and out deeply until you feel relaxed. Bring your attention to your head and notice any tension you may be feeling in your forehead, eyes, cheeks, and so on, and release or let go of it. Once you have done this, bring your attention to your neck and shoulders; again, notice any tension you may be feeling and release or let go of it in the same way you did with your head. Slowly work through each body part in turn, from the top half of your body right through to your toes. Make sure you release any stress or tension as you go. By the time you reach your toes you should be feeling totally relaxed.

You may notice your Inner Critic popping up to remind you of all the things you need to do. It might point out that you have an itchy foot or a tickle in your throat; it might remind you that you don't have time for this nonsense and tell you to get up and do something more useful. This is normal, even when you've been practising meditation for a long time. Recognize this voice and visualize shutting it outside the door, or imagine putting it in a box and locking it in there with a key. Sometimes it may take quite a while for this negative voice to dissipate, so be patient and give yourself time. Repetition is the key to mastering meditation.

Stay in this relaxed state for as long as you want. Enjoy the peace until you feel ready to come back to the room again.

Mantra

Take up your chosen position, close your eyes, relax and start noticing your breathing – breathe in and out deeply. Notice any repetitive thoughts and, as they pop into your head, release them in a way that works for you. Maybe imagine bursting them as you would a balloon, or put your unwanted thoughts in a box, or just imagine pressing the 'delete' key in your own head. Keep doing this until you feel your mind empty.

When you are ready, repeat your chosen mantra over and over again, slowly and concisely. Concentrate on the words as you say them. Here are some sample mantras:

- *'Om' or 'Aum' is the most common and significant word in mantra tradition. It is considered as the root mantra of all mantras, but you can of course make up your own.*

- *I am love.*

- *I let go and I am free.*

- *I deserve only the best.*

- *I give and receive love.*

- *I release all anxiety and fear.*

- *I allow love to flow within me.*

Stay in this relaxed state for as long as you want. Enjoy the peace until you feel ready to return to the room again.

White Light

Take up your chosen position and close your eyes, relax and start noticing your breathing – breathe in and out deeply. Notice any repetitive thoughts and, as they pop into your head, release them in a way that works for you. As with the mantra above, burst them as you would a balloon, lock them in a box or press the 'delete' key in your head. Keep doing this until you feel your mind empty.

Now I want you to imagine in your mind's eye a large beam of bright pure white light cascading into the top of your head. Make the pure white light as bright as you possibly can. See the white light penetrating your head and clearing out any negative thoughts and beliefs. See the white light work its way through your entire body, washing away any unwanted energy. Once you have allowed this pure white light to penetrate your whole body, imagine it now forming a ball of light around your body, almost like a protective energy field that nothing can penetrate. Allow yourself to bask in this pure white light for as long as you need to.

Stay in this relaxed state for as long as you want to. Enjoy the peace until you feel ready to come back to the room again.

Spend the next week trying out these three different techniques to see which one you prefer. Commit to meditating at least once a day for 30 days and see what a difference it makes.

VISUALIZATION

I first stumbled upon visualization early on in my journey and started using it immediately, with remarkable results. Visualization is nothing new and has been taught by leading teachers and avatars for countless generations.

As mentioned in Chapter 2, some of the world's most successful people use visualization as part of their everyday lives. Every successful person will tell you the same thing: she could see her success long before it actually happened! Visualization is one of the most effective ways of manifesting your dreams and goals. Whatever you picture in your mind, you are on some level creating for yourself. The fact is that most of us unconsciously use this remarkable ability to imagine negative things happening to us instead of consciously focusing on what we actually *want* to happen.

Visualization is the technique of using your conscious mind to make your subconscious mind aware of all of your dreams and desires. Everyone's mind works on two different levels; using visualization will help you to get both parts of your mind working in synchrony. The conscious mind is the logical, 'thinking' mind that you are aware of and use every day. It is under your control and creates your thoughts. Your thoughts influence how you feel and what actions you take, and the results that you get. Most of us focus our attention on the conscious mind when we are trying to achieve a particular goal. We make plans and we try to think positively, but somehow we still fail. Using just the conscious mind alone will get you nowhere fast. The secret to getting results is to use the *sub*conscious mind as well! All of our emotions, experiences and beliefs are nicely tucked away in our subconscious mind, and we are completely unaware of most of them. This is the 'feeling' part of the mind and it influences our conscious thoughts and behaviours. Simply put, your subconscious mind is where all your 'programming' takes place. Visualization helps you to tap into your subconscious and change the old programming that is stopping your goals, dreams or desires coming to fruition. So when you have both parts of your mind working together, you will achieve success much more easily.

Many experiments have been carried out into the power of positive visualization. Scientists have linked an Olympic sprinter up to biofeedback equipment so they could monitor his brain activity. They then asked the athlete to sprint around a track as if he were running an actual race, and then asked him to run the same race in his head while sitting in a chair linked to the same biofeedback equipment. Amazingly, the scientists found that the same brain activity was generated when the athlete actually ran the race as when he ran it in his head. So what does this tell us? That the sprinter's brain couldn't tell the difference between running the race physically and running it in his mind – to his brain, the power of the imagined race was as real as the actual race.

What most of us don't realize is that all of creation (including our own lives) starts from within our own mind. We are so misled that we believe we must change our outward circumstances in order to change our lives, when in fact we need first to go within. When you are visualizing you are changing the programming of your mind. You are changing unwanted thoughts, beliefs, habits and behaviours, and are 'rewiring' your brain! Remember, you are just a mass of electrical circuits, but if you have some faulty wiring you can change it by using mental images and pictures. The reason why visualization is so successful is that when you practise it, you are creating vivid pictures in your mind's eye of yourself with what it is you desire, whether that's better health, a more loving relationship, a new car, a better job or more money. You generate new, positive thoughts, feelings and beliefs that help re-programme your mind. You also invoke the Law of Attraction to help you manifest what it is you want. And that's when miracles start happening!

All success starts from within. Like Thomas Edison and the lightbulb or Alexander Graham Bell and the telephone, you will see your success in your mind long before you actually succeed in reality. Remember, visualization is the field where everything is created!

Let me demonstrate. I want you to close your eyes (once you've read this, of course!) and imagine you're holding a juicy ripe lemon in your hand. The lemon is a vibrant yellow and its skin is bumpy to the touch. It has just come out of the fridge and feels cold in the palm of your hand. Even though the fruit has not been cut, you can smell it. Imagine picking up a knife and slicing the lemon in half on a kitchen work surface. As you do this, citrus juices spurt out and some of the juice runs on to your finger. You put both the knife and the lemon down and quickly lick the juice off your hand. It's terribly sour!

Is your mouth watering yet?

What this little exercise demonstrates is that using the power of your imagination you can stimulate your saliva glands without even tasting the fruit for real. So if your imagination can do this, what else it is capable of generating?

The first thing I noticed when I started visualizing was how enjoyable it was, like a wonderful daydream that I rarely wanted to end. It was really pleasurable, mainly because I was in control of the images I created in my head and, of course, precisely because I was in control I was able to ensure that all the 'movies' I would play out were positive, fun and exhilarating, where only good things happened to me. It was like being the director of my own movie.

When I first started visualizing, I was in a job that I didn't particularly enjoy. I never seemed to have enough time, my savings were minimal and I didn't feel as if I was being the best mother I could be. There was plenty of room for improvement in my life at that time, and I had lots of ideas of how I wanted my life to look instead. At that time I'd arrive home at 6 p.m. each night. I would bathe my daughter, feed her dinner and tuck her up safely in bed. I would then rummage through the freezer to find something I could cook for my partner and myself with the least amount of effort possible. My life was hectic, and deep down I was desperate for change.

Even though it would have been easier to just flop onto the sofa with a huge glass of wine, I would summon up the energy to spend 10 minutes meditating, followed by a further 15 minutes of visualizing – every evening without fail. I would visualize myself doing a job I thoroughly enjoyed (even though I had no idea what that job was). I would see myself sitting in my home office, which hadn't even been built, working away on a computer I hadn't even bought yet. I would observe myself typing away, no idea what I was writing but I would feel a sense of satisfaction and fulfilment from the work I was doing. I would visualize checking my bank account and smiling as I looked at a healthy balance. It felt wonderful. I'd look around at my happy home with lots of space and beautiful new furniture. I'd see all the DIY completed and notice how all my cupboards were neatly displayed with everything in place. I would look outside and see my fine-looking vegetable garden lush with fresh green salads and herbs, and I would see my daughter playing barefoot on the daisy-laden grass. I would see myself having time to peruse my many cookbooks and prepare nutritious meals for my family. I saw myself having regular dinner parties and playing the perfect hostess. I pictured myself having time to enjoy my daughter to the full, bathing her, playing with her and reading her endless stories. Bliss! I saw my life exactly how I wanted it to be. And I did this consistently every night, month after month after month, even when there was no inkling of change on the horizon.

Things didn't really start changing until almost six months into this process. To see results takes time, and everything depends on how much you're willing to commit. The more you put in, the more you get out. I started to notice changes happening: opportunities and ideas came into my awareness, along with new people, new possibilities and new information. I wish I could say that one day I woke up with my fairy godmother at my side and living my dream life, but it wasn't quite that simple.

Where would be the fun in that?! I had to get off my backside and take opportunities as they presented themselves to me. Slowly but surely, things started to alter. The changes didn't always happen in the way I expected, but my life did start to expand. It wasn't until almost two years later, on a beautiful summer afternoon when I was sitting in my new dining room (recently built) writing an article for a magazine, that I suddenly became aware of the journey I had taken. There I was: I had given up my marketing job and had set up my own business as a life-coach. I had more time to spend with my family and do the things I truly enjoyed. And I had even planted my own vegetable patch! It was a moment I will never forget. In those few seconds I realized my power. *I* had created the life I was living, no one else but me! I had created it, not by trying to force things to change, but by going within. The more I committed to my inner world, the more joy I experienced in my outer world. It was that simple!

The most common thing I encounter when teaching people about visualization is that most people don't believe in their own imagination. These days we tend to use our intellect far more than our imagination or intuition. We think too much, we try to be logical and rationalize everything until we can make sense of it. Everything that remains unexplained is simply dismissed because it cannot be proven. But, as mentioned earlier, science is starting to uncover some new truths about the human mind and spirit.

Our imagination is the medium through which we focus our mental energy to create our own happiness or hardship in this world. Once we grasp this, our lives will really start to transform.

The great thing with visualization is that you can be your own scientist. Try it and see for yourself. My only disclaimer is this: first, you must be clear about your desired outcome (your goals) and, second, you must commit to a set period of time. There is no point trying once, twice or even five times, because it's simply not enough. Commit for 5 minutes a day for three months. Let's face it, 5 minutes a day just before you go to sleep is hardly asking too much. Is it?

Tips When Using Visualization

- *Practise*. Repetition is the key to any new skill.

- *See yourself in the third person*, as if you were watching a film and you were the lead actor, or as if you were outside yourself looking on.

- *Put emotions into it*. Feel how great it would feel to have achieved your goals.

- *Make it real*. See the colours, imagine the smells and sounds; make the scene as real as possible.

- *Keep it positive*. Do not let negative thoughts or feelings in while visualizing.

Here are four different visualizations for you to try.

1. Seeing into Your Future

This is the exercise I used to manifest the changes in my life. Try it, but remember: to see the effects you must commit to practising it every day.

Find somewhere you can relax, perhaps sitting in your favourite chair or lying on your bed. Make yourself comfortable and start breathing in and out deeply until you feel your body relax. When you're ready, close your eyes.

Once you are ready I want you to imagine how you want your life to be, approximately one year into the future. Focus as much as you can on the detail, using sound, colour, touch and taste in your daydream. Make the picture bright, vivid and as real as possible. Notice how you look, what are you wearing? Notice your surroundings, what are they like? Where are you? What is the weather like today? With whom are you sharing your day? How will you be spending your evening? What are you doing for a living and what is it you enjoy most about your work? How do you feel about your financial situation? Spend some time looking back at the previous year: what are you most proud of achieving? What is it you now believe about yourself? How do you feel about this?

Once you're happy you've spent enough time living in your future, slowly bring your attention back to your surroundings. Smile and know your desired future is yours for the taking.

2. Self-healing

Whether you're as healthy as an ox or you're currently feeling unwell, visualization has been proved to be extremely powerful at aiding recovery, be it from a common cold or more serious illness.

Find somewhere you can relax. Make yourself comfortable and start breathing in and out deeply until you feel your body relax. When you're ready, close your eyes.

Imagine your immune system in a way that resonates with you: perhaps you see lots of bulldozers driving around your body; maybe you find it easier to visualize a triumphant army marching through your system, or maybe you see lots of tiny little fish swimming through your bloodstream. It doesn't really matter what you choose. Now, imagine your illness (whatever that may be) as a dark grey area within your body. Notice its size and location. Visualize your chosen immune system warriors and see them saturating the dark grey area; see this area reducing in size – becoming smaller and smaller until you cannot see it any more.

Once you have done this, mentally thank your immune system for its sterling job and send it back on its way to patrolling your body, protecting it from further invasion. Finally, I want you now to see and feel your body as healed and healthy.

When you're ready, slowly bring your attention back to your surroundings. Smile and know that your body is completely healthy. Feel the difference!

3. The Real You

This exercise is good at increasing confidence and self-esteem, and is a great way to start your day. You will recognize that it's a variation of the exercise we did in Chapter 4 (see page 88).

Find somewhere you can relax and make yourself comfortable. Start breathing deeply in and out until you feel your body relax. When you're ready, close your eyes.

Imagine another 'you' standing in front of you. This is your 'perfect' you. This is the 'you' that has already achieved all your goals. Look at your body and admire all the things you like: look at your hair and skin, and notice how healthy they look. This is your true self and the most wonderful version of 'you' that you can imagine.

Now notice how your true self stands, talks, moves; notice the confidence that oozes out of your body. Notice how relaxed and comfortable your other self is. Your true self has achieved everything you have ever wanted or dreamed of. What advice does the real you want to share with you?

I want you now to imagine stepping into your true self's body so that your two bodies have now become one. Notice the difference in how you feel. Look through the eyes of your true self: what do you see? How are things different? Now let your mind wander and imagine all the things you would do if you were living in your true self's body all the time. What differences would occur? What would you spend your time doing? How would you feel? When you feel this new confidence flowing through your body, slowly bring your attention back to your surroundings.

4. Create Your Ideal Day

This exercise is a good way to start each and every day. Try it for a week and see what happens.

Find somewhere you can relax. Make yourself comfortable and start breathing in and out deeply until you feel your body relax. When you're ready, close your eyes.

Mentally take note of all the wonderful things you already have in your life – from your home, friends, family, your health or perhaps your material possessions. Note everything you have to be grateful for, big or small. Leave nothing out! See yourself carrying out all your normal activities and talking to your family, friends and colleagues. See how wonderful your day is, and how smoothly it runs. Notice how self-assured you are and how happy you feel. Take a couple of minutes to plan your day, exactly as you want it to go.

When you're ready, slowly bring your attention back to your surroundings. Have a wonderful day!

Spend the next week trying out these four different visualizations to see which one you prefer. Commit to visualizing at least once a day for 30 days and see what difference it makes.

THE POWER OF PRAYER

Although I don't follow a particular religion, I am a huge advocate of the power of prayer. I grew up with religious roots, mainly from my mother's upbringing as a Catholic, and while we rarely went to church other than at Christmas and Easter time, I was brought up always to say my prayers every night before going to bed. For me, praying wasn't so much a religious ritual but more an ingrained habit or obligation. In a way it was like brushing my teeth or taking a shower. It wasn't until I jumped onto my spiritual path that I truly understood its true meaning and power. Prayer, like meditation and visualization, is just another method of going within and connecting to your inner spirit.

There have been many studies into the power of prayer and meditation, and recent research work has shown that people who either pray, or are prayed for, recover far more quickly from illness than those who do not or are not.

For me, prayer is just a direct connection to spirit, to my true self. When you connect with this part of yourself you are using the power of your all-fulfilling spirit to create the life you were always meant to live until your mental programming took hold of you. I find it a wonderful support, almost like I have a best friend to share my life with: *someone who is always there and is never judgemental or critical.*

It is my belief that through meditation, visualization and prayer we are connecting with our inner spirit, God or whatever name you wish to call 'it', and when we do this we transcend all material baggage and negative beliefs, habits and behaviours. Connecting regularly with our spirit will help us to re-programme our minds; all we have to do is make a commitment to 'hook up' as much as possible through whichever means works for us.

How do you pray? Well, however you want to. There are no hard-and-fast rules. When I pray it's just like I'm having a friendly conversation with my Inner Guide. I tell my Inner Guide about all my concerns and worries, and ask for new insights and ideas to present themselves to me. It's just like talking to an old friend.

Pray to whomever or whatever feels comfortable – perhaps God, your Inner Guide or maybe a relative. If it feels right to you, you cannot go wrong.

CONNECTING MIND, BODY AND SPIRIT

What I have come to realize is that we are all made up of three different levels: body, mind, and spirit. The body is made up of all our skin, muscles, organs, blood, bones, cells and so on. Our mind is made up of billions of neuro-pathways and circuits, where all our programming is stored just like a computer hard drive. Our spirit is that part of us that is eternal pure energy. Science has spent the last 200 years or so investigating the body. We understand more now than we have ever done about human anatomy. Science has also made huge advances during the last 30 years or so in studying the power of the mind and the way our brains operate. Our spirit, on the other hand, is yet to be understood fully by the scientific community. Things such as the Law of Attraction, the afterlife and God are still mysteries and are often dispelled because of a lack of evidence to support them.

> *Science is uncovering truths about the human race that will turn our current reality on its head. But remember, just because you don't understand something doesn't mean it's not true. It's all part of evolution: truth changes!*

The Victorians would have been amazed by the concept of mobile phones, jet aircraft or the World

Wide Web. Look how much has changed! Look how technology has advanced. Science has reached a turning-point. We have locked ourselves in our current paradigm and haven't even considered that there might be a better way. Truth changes and so does scientific fact. *How can a fish know it is in water? To a fish no other reality is imaginable!*

When we live our lives using only body and mind alone, we find ourselves struggling. Our bodies let us down and life seems to be inconsistent and complicated. We've been misled. We've all been missing a crucial piece of the jigsaw! We are so much more than our bodies and minds; we are also spiritual beings. When we can start nurturing the spiritual side of ourselves, our lives become a joy to live. How? I'm not quite sure, but when you combine all three aspects of yourself – mind, body and spirit – miracles start to unfold in your life.

As we continue through the remainder of this book I want you to make a commitment to start nurturing your inner spirit in a way that feels right for you. If you do this you will find that your journey to living a wonderful life will be smoother, easier and more enjoyable. Achieving your goals will become effortless. Don't get me wrong: there are lots of people who are hugely successful utilizing their body and mind alone to achieve their endeavours, but what I'm saying is that by adding the third element (your spirit), your journey will blessed in every way possible. Instead of fighting your way through the jungle single-handed, you will receive an unearthly support that only spirit can provide. Things will fall into place with a minimal amount of effort. Circumstances will present themselves at the perfect time, and the right people will come into your life just when you need them most. Isn't this the way it's supposed to be? Why would you want to struggle when you don't have to?!

When life gets tough or complicated it's a huge warning sign that we've lost our connection with spirit. When things start going in the wrong direction, it's time to stop and go within. If you can stay connected regularly you will lead an enchanted life. You will become one of those people about whom others say, 'What is it she does that's different to me?'

How do you stay connected? Through deter-mination and commitment: you cannot expect to go to the gym for a month and have the perfect physique for the rest of your life, that's just crazy! The more you connect with your inner spirit, the more joy and pleasure you will receive in your day-to-day life. You need to create a daily routine or ritual of going within, via whatever method works best for you. Maybe that's meditation, perhaps spending lots of time in Nature, with animals, or maybe through visualization or prayer. Find a method of connection that works for you. You will know what feels right.

Exercise

Over the next month make sure you connect with your spirit on a daily basis. Even 5 minutes a day will do. The more you connect, the better results you will get.

YOUR HOMEPLAY THIS WEEK

1. Open your eyes this week to the true wonderment of the world around you.

2. Try meditating for 5 minutes every day for the next week and notice what changes occur.

3. Visualize your future as you would want it to be. Start off small by visualizing your day in advance, and build on from there.

CHAPTER 7

The Real Secrets of Making It Happen

Congratulations! You're almost there and have arrived at the final two chapters of the book. Let's review your journey so far. In the first few chapters we took time to explore what was currently going on in your life, and looked at all the potential areas for change. I then encouraged you to expand your comfort zone and start thinking about setting some big, juicy, life-changing goals. Chapters 3 and 4 took you on an inward journey into the workings of your mind, and we crept inside dark crevasses of your psyche, looking for all the outdated programming and how it is affecting or will continue to affect your life if you don't do something about it. And, more importantly, I shared with you my best tips and techniques for adopting a fresh new attitude; these will not only help you achieve wonderful things, they will also assist you in making your comfort zone far wider than ever before. Finally I took you on a spiritual journey into the realms of 'energy', and we looked at the Law of Attraction, at meditation and visualization.

You've done all the required work beneath the surface and I think it's about time you got into action! Let's face it, if you really want to make some big changes to your life, you're going to have to get out there and start making it happen. And that's exactly what we are going to do now. And, yes, it means you are going to have to *do* something!

In this chapter I'm going to show you the nitty-gritty of how to transfer your goals from paper to reality. I'm going to show you everything you need to know to make sure you reach your desired target, whether that is to secure a promotion, to change careers completely, to start your own business, meet someone special, re-invent yourself, reach spiritual enlightenment, get fit or become financially free. Whatever your goal, the process is the same.

It's time to dig out the three goals you set yourself way back in Chapter 2. But, before you go any further, and because it has been a while since you set your goals, I want you to ask yourself the following questions again:

- Are these really my goals?

- Am I committed to achieving these goals?

- Do these goals excite me?

- Will achieving these goals make me feel happy?

It's vitally important that you set the right goals, because if you don't you're setting yourself up to fail. How do you know if you've set the right goals?

- You feel extremely excited and scared at the same time.

- You can't seem to focus on anything because you are too busy daydreaming.

- You feel impatient and immediately start researching your goals.

- You wake up in the morning and, for the first time in years, you have a smile on your face.

If you're still unsure about whether you've set the right goals, go back and read Chapter 2 again or, alternatively, get someone to give you a hand.

TAKING RESPONSIBILITY

I hope you are starting to realize that *no one but you* is responsible for your life. It really is time to grow up and stop blaming your parents, your job, your partner or the state of the economy for the way your life is. It's time to stand on your own two feet and start building the life you deserve because, believe me, if you don't do it, no one else will! Every successful person knows this truth. If you think writing your goals down is enough to make them manifest, you're deluding yourself. There is no fairy godmother out there to wave her magic wand and make your dreams all come true before your eyes. If, secretly, this is what you're waiting for, you're going to be waiting for a long time.

Remember, you're your own fairy godmother!

There is nothing worse than living with regret. I'd hate to be 80 years old and wish I had written a book, started a business, run a marathon for charity, manufactured that product, met the right partner, had children, lost weight or whatever. Living with regret is excruciating and fills us with profound disappointment.

No more excuses, no more procrastinating. Your future is in your hands!

I often meet people who, when I ask: 'What do you want to do with the rest of your life?' tell me about their dreams and ambitions, but as soon as the words leave their mouths they bombard me with copious reasons as to why these things won't – or can't – happen. They tell me, 'I'd love to retrain as a teacher, but I'm too much in debt' or 'I'd love to open my own café, but I'm not clever enough and wouldn't have a clue where to start.' These are excuses. I remember when I decided to retrain and become a life-coach; I was so excited I could hardly contain my enthusiasm. I knew I would have to retrain and I knew it would cost me money, but I wasn't prepared for the shock I received when I found out just how much my training would cost. How on Earth was I going to afford it? I had a little money saved in the bank, but nowhere near enough. My Inner Critic revelled in the news and flooded my mind with thoughts such as, 'Oh, well, it was a nice idea' and 'You wouldn't have succeeded anyway.' The next morning I awoke with two choices: either I would forget the whole thing or I would throw caution to the wind and follow my dream, whatever the expense. I made my choice, and thank goodness I did. It wasn't easy, but it has been life-changing. It was the best decision I ever made. Sometimes we just have to take a risk. How easy it would have been for me to remain within my comfort zone and continue to let the Inner Critic rule my life. Yes, very easy. But if I hadn't made the decision to start afresh I would probably still be where I was seven years ago, and that thought just fills me with dread.

START BELIEVING YOUR GOALS ARE POSSIBLE

Let's get clear about something: if you are going to achieve your goals, you're going to need to start believing that they are feasible. If you have any doubts whatsoever, you are simply going to slow yourself down or, worse still, you will set yourself up to fail. It's essential that you implement the right beliefs to ensure your victory. If you put your mind to it you can change anything in your life: your job, your relationship, your health, your home, your financial status, your stress levels. But you must start believing it's possible.

In order to make a start, let's recapitulate the previous chapters and start employing the techniques we've covered so far:

- Create new affirmations for each goal you have set, and start repeating them to yourself on a daily basis.

- Create a 'vision board' containing all the images and photographs you can find which represent the life you are aspiring to.

- Research others who have successfully walked the path before you, and read inspiring autobiographies or other 'self-help' or spiritual books.

- Tune in to your Inner Guide as much as you can and listen for the messages that are given to you.

- Meditate daily and ensure you regularly visualize your future exactly as you want it, by using the examples in Chapter 6.

- Most importantly, as you start moving towards your goals, begin creating your list of evidence, as this will be undeniable proof that your beliefs are starting to change.

If you do all of these things your beliefs will, without doubt, start to alter.

When I started my voyage to becoming a life-coach, like most of us my self-belief was limited. I had lots of doubts and fears, which only began to alter when I started practising the techniques listed above. On my car journey to work I would switch off the radio and use the 20-minute drive to repeat my affirmations over and over again, and on the way home I would listen to inspirational audio tapes from well-known authors from around the world. At work I would often nip off to the Ladies' and take time for 2- or 3-minute 'mini-meditations'. When I arrived home I would then find the time to meditate and visualize my life as I wanted it. I spent every spare moment with my nose in self-help books and would read one book every week, adopting any new methods that I thought were useful.

I was totally serious about changing my life. My commitment and determination were irrefutable. I completely saturated myself in anything and everything that I could find which would help me to create the right mindset and, ultimately, help me to achieve my goals.

Exercise

Ask yourself: what are the three things I am going to do from now on that will help me to start believing my goals are possible?

GETTING OUT OF YOUR COMFORT ZONE

A prerequisite to achieving your goals is leaving your comfort zone, and that is going to feel uncomfortable. Most of us live our lives nicely 'tucked in' within our self-created comfort zones. Although a nice, quiet, uneventful life without turbulence or unrest may sound lovely, it's unlikely. We all have to face change throughout our lives, whether we like it or not. We have two choices: either to instigate the change or wait for it to be forced upon us. I know which one I'd rather choose. Life isn't about avoiding change at all costs, or about wrapping yourself up in cotton wool; this is no way to exist and you'll end up growing old with many disappointments and regrets.

In order to grow and expand, we need to experience new things, and when we do so, new opportunities arise, new people walk into our lives and fresh doors open up for us to walk through.

I believe that each one of us is programmed to look for ways of enriching or 'upgrading' who we are. Deep down we all want more, we all want to feel satisfied and we all want to be happy. But to do so we need to leave the familiar boundaries of our comfort zone. And you know what? It's never as bad as you imagine it's going to be! We'll talk more about facing your fears in the final chapter.

Exercise

List five things you can do this week that will push you to expand your comfort zone – from driving a new route to work or buying clothing in a colour you wouldn't normally wear to making that phone call you've been putting off for weeks. I promise you'll feel fantastic with your achievements.

WHO SETS GOALS?

Most people think goals are actually glorified New Year's resolutions. And for most of us, this is true. It has been said that only 3 per cent of the population set goals for themselves – but those who do are among the wealthiest in the country.

How many of us have made a New Year's resolution either to stop smoking, stop eating chocolate, stop drinking, get out of debt, find love or whatever, only to find out that by the 20th of January we've forgotten all about it? Most of us drift haphazardly from one year to the next; never really stopping to see whether we're travelling in the right direction. Try this analogy: you go into a restaurant, have a look at the menu and within a few minutes decide what you fancy. The waiter takes your order and you relax, knowing full well that your food is on its way. But what if you went into the restaurant and told the waiter you were hungry but couldn't decide what to order? How could the waiter bring you your food? You would remain hungry! It's the same with life: we remain unfulfilled if we don't decide what it is that we want.

It's easy to see the absurdity of the behaviour in the analogy, yet most of us act like this when dealing with our lives. If you want to steer your life in the right direction you've to grab hold of the menu and start deciding what you want, because if you don't you'll either remain hungry or someone else will order for you and you may not like what you get.

It has been proved that those who set goals achieve far greater things than those who don't. When you think about this, it makes complete sense. When you have a target in front of you, you become incredibly focused and determined. Think about a time in your life when this was true for you.

Achieving your targets or goals feels truly amazing. It keeps you moving forwards from one goal to the next. As soon as you reach one goal you are looking for the next challenge, your next 'achievement fix'. And through this process your self-belief increases and your confidence soars. This is why some of the people our society sees as successful – people such as

Donald Trump, Alan Sugar, Bill Gates or Madonna, for example – strive always to continue to achieve. They didn't make it to their first goal and then decide that was it; they used the momentum of achievement to carry them forwards. Once you start goal-setting, you, too, will find this is true.

WHY PEOPLE DON'T ACHIEVE THEIR GOALS

There are a few crucial mistakes that people make when setting goals. First, people set too small a goal. A client came to see me insisting that one of her key goals was to book a summer holiday to Greece, even though she went abroad every year. Now this is all very well, but when I asked the client if the holiday would happen anyway, regardless of her working with me or not, she stuttered and agreed it would. She didn't need a life-coach to help her book a holiday that was going to happen anyway. Remember, your goals must be big enough to take you out of your comfort zone. When I probed a little further it turned out that the client had always wanted to run in the London Marathon in aid of the charity Breast Cancer Care. Now there's a more challenging goal if ever I heard one! Goals must be big enough to excite you but fill you with fear at the same time – that's when you know your comfort zone is being stretched. Setting too small a goal might well be comfortable, but it's just a cop-out! You're fooling yourself.

Conversely, people also tend to set themselves goals that are too big – goals so gigantic that even the world's most adept goal-reacher might struggle to achieve them. They set themselves up to fail right from the start. Yes, your goals must stretch you, but they must also be realistic. If someone came to me wanting to earn a million pounds within one month, I would have to ask whether this goal was really achievable and, if so, on what basis. There is absolutely nothing wrong with setting yourself a big goal like this, but I would suggest breaking it down into manageable chunks and setting a pragmatic deadline.

Remember, your goals should be attainable within a six-month period. If you're unsure whether your goal is too big or too small, re-read Chapter 2 for clarification.

People also tend to overlook the need to break their goals down into manageable, bite-sized pieces, leaving them feeling completely confused and overwhelmed. One of the most important things you do when working with a life-coach is to analyse your goals and then break them down into smaller portions and deal with one portion at a time. This way you don't allow yourself to become weighed down or besieged.

Another major pitfall is not doing the internal work required, such as getting the right mindset or attitude. As mentioned before, if you are harbouring negative beliefs towards your goal, no matter how hard you try to push or force things to happen, you will remain in the same loop.

Remember, what you believe, on some level becomes your reality.

If you believe your goals aren't achievable, they won't be. This is why it is important not to set too big a goal. If you want to achieve your goals you must do the internal work as well.

Finally, people set themselves up to fail by telling too many people about their dreams and ambitions. I know when you get an incredible idea the first thing you want to do is share it with those you love – it's only natural. But, as much as people care about us, they can pour icy cold water over our ideas. I call them 'dream-stealers'. Why? Well, it's not because they don't love us or that they think our idea is rubbish; it's because they're worried we might be disappointed, and because our ambition highlights their own imperfections or lack of drive to live the life they want for themselves. In short, people feel bad if you're taking control of *your* life and they're not in charge of theirs. I have clients come to me, having set wonderful, life-changing goals in their initial session, only to find that they come back the following week wanting to downsize their ideas. When I ask why, it's invariably because they've talked it through with their partner, friends, mum or siblings, who, in turn, have led the client to believe that maybe the goal is a bit too far-fetched or unrealistic. This subsequently influences the mindset of the clients and their ability to believe in themselves.

Do *not* let other people smother your dreams. Keep your light under a bushel. Be selective about whom you share your dream and ideas with. We'll talk about this further in a moment.

HOW TO MAKE IT HAPPEN

There are six primary elements to accomplishing your goals:

1. Break your goals down into strategies
2. Take consistent weekly action
3. Create a support network
4. Become accountable
5. Keep the excitement alive
6. Don't tell the world.

Let's look at each one of these in more detail.

1. Break Your Goals Down into Strategies

Once you have established your goals, you need to take each one in turn and divide it into smaller chunks. I call these chunks 'strategies' or 'milestones'. By doing this you don't become overwhelmed by the magnitude of the journey on which you're about to embark. Once we allow ourselves to become overwhelmed we start procrastinating and postponing our actions. This invariably means that our goals never even make it off the ground.

Look at it like this: if I said to you 'I want to drive from London to Madrid in one day, in one continuous journey without stopping or slowing down,' would it be realistic? Of course not. But if I were to say, 'I want to drive from London to Madrid over three days, and stop off in Paris, Bordeaux and Zaragoza before finally reaching Madrid on the third day,' how realistic is this? You cannot expect to complete your journey overnight. It takes time. And if you want to be successful you must break your goal down into milestones. For example, running a marathon may well seem impossible until you have broken it down into manageable chunks of, first, running 3 miles, then 7, then 12, then 18 before finally moving to the full 26. During this process you're building strength and stamina (both physically and mentally), which will guarantee your personal victory. Without strategies you simply won't know where to start.

> *Having a clear plan of action will put you on the most efficient path to achieving your goals.*

When we don't set a clear plan of action we jump ahead of ourselves, causing ourselves more work in the long term.

Setting your strategies is straightforward, but it might be worth getting someone to help you, as no doubt he or she will think of things you won't. Sit down with a blank piece of paper and brainstorm all the major areas you think you'll need to cover in order to reach each of your goals. Don't worry about the order at this stage; just list everything that comes to mind. Remember, you're not listing physical actions (that will come later); you're putting together an inventory of the main areas you're going to need to cover on your journey. I suggest setting between three and eight strategies for each of your goals. If you find you have a list of nine or more, refine and amalgamate your list until you have no more than eight. Say you were planning your wedding day, for instance. As I'm sure you can imagine, there are a million and one things to do before the big day arrives. So rather than getting yourself bogged down you would create a series of milestones to cover, one at a time, putting them into the order in which they'd need to be tackled. For example, your strategy list might include: the venue, catering, theme, outfits, guest list, transport and honeymoon. This breaks the whole goal down into manageable pieces and it becomes less of a monster to tackle. You then concentrate on one strategy at a time. You do not move on to your next strategy until you've finished working on your current one. This way you're taking smaller steps towards your goal, rather than going round in circles. Remember, *you eat an elephant one mouthful at a time!*

Here are three examples of goals and how your strategies might look.

Goal: To go on a once-in-a-lifetime holiday around the world next summer

- Establish resources.

- Decide on the locations.

- Look at finances.

- Devise a timetable.

- Book holiday.

- Prepare for leaving.

Goal: To increase my self-esteem so I can meet someone special by Christmas

- Look at beliefs and behaviours.

- Research new techniques to change mindset.

- Adopt techniques.

- Change mindset.

- Look at ways of meeting new people and expanding social network.

- Start dating.

Goal: To find a career I'm truly passionate about by March

- Establish likes and dislikes of current career.

- Look at values and passions.

- Define natural abilities and talents.

- Look at all career options.

- Decide on three career paths to research.

- Decide on one path to pursue.

- Start training.

2. Take Consistent Weekly Action

Once you've created your strategies, it's time to get into action. This is the point where you need to get off the sofa, go out there and start bringing your goals to life.

You could plan and strategize until the cows come home but this won't change your life a jot.

Actions are the key to success! They are the engine to your dreams.

You set actions by taking each strategy in turn and creating a series of small steps. I would recommend setting three or four actions every day, from making a phone call or arranging a meeting to carrying out research. If you were to take three or four actions every day, that's 20 actions per week, which takes you 20 steps closer to your goal. If you keep this momentum up you'll achieve your goals in record time. Keep your strategies to hand when planning your actions, as they are your overall road map leading you to your desired destination; remember only to set actions around your current strategy – tempting as it may be, don't jump ahead!

Perhaps you could sit down every Sunday night and write a 'to do' list of all the actions you intend to take in the week ahead. Sunday night might be 'planning' night. It ensures that every Monday morning you wake up full of enthusiasm and passion. You never, ever, feel directionless when you have a 'to do' list to work through. And the best thing is having the satisfaction of crossing off items as you do them! Get into the habit of doing this and you're on the road to victory.

There is one final ingredient to setting actions: remember to follow the signs the universe provides. If you're regularly connecting, through whatever means is right for you, setting your actions should be effortless and easy. The universe provides the clues you need to follow, but you must be awake in order to pick them up.

3. Create a Support Network

It's important to create a network of people around you who can help you along on your journey. So who do you know who may help you attain your goals? Go through your mobile phone, your email address book or old diaries and social networking sites and see who in your network has the potential to assist you. Maybe it's an old work colleague who now works in a field similar to the one you want to move into. Perhaps a friend who works for a newspaper can get you the publicity you need, or maybe you know someone who has just been on a workshop that would be perfect for you. Open your eyes and look around you: you'll be amazed at the resources you have at your fingertips. If you don't know anyone, ask around, look on the internet and make a few telephone calls. Reading a good book may also be a tremendous source of support. I have read some truly amazing books and without the wisdom of their authors I wouldn't be where I am today.

4. Become Accountable

This is an extremely important component of getting to where you want to be. How many of us have real accountability in our lives? Most of us stopped being answerable to anyone the day we hung up our school uniforms for the last time. Let's face it: we are a nation of procrastinators. If there is no one to push us forwards we remain within our comfort zone where it is nice and safe. Once I had a taskmaster of a boss: he always had his beady eye on me, watching my every move and making sure I was working to my full capacity. Although I absolutely hated this at the time, there is no doubt whatsoever that I worked harder when he was in the office. When he went out, which he did frequently, I'd slow down my pace considerably. Funny, that! It's just like having a personal trainer.

When you have someone standing by your side encouraging and pushing you, you're more likely to do 50 bench-presses than 30!

I'm not suggesting that you find someone who will berate you every time you find yourself dragging your feet, but a good, healthy dose of accountability will certainly help you achieve far greater things and, more importantly, you'll reach your goals much more quickly. This is exactly why coaching works so well. A survey by the International Coaching Federation revealed that 98.5 per cent of clients polled reported their investment in coaching to be highly valuable. The general feedback from clients was that using a coach enabled them to become incredibly focused and therefore produce results faster. Accountability works!

It's time to create your 'coaching buddy'. To whom can you become accountable? Having someone impartial such as a life-coach or mentor is always advantageous, but I understand that this isn't always an option for everyone, so consider a family member, colleague or good friend. Choose your coaching buddy carefully, as you need someone who will support you fully and not water down your plan.

The job of your coaching buddy is to:

- give you undivided support at all times

- praise you when things go well

- encourage you when you hit obstacles

- commit to having a weekly conversation with you to ensure that you are keeping on track

- celebrate your successes with you.

To get your coaching buddy to 'buy-in' to your goals, you need to tell him or her about your overall plan and what you expect your coaching buddy to do. He or she needs to know exactly what the coaching buddy's role is in helping you achieve your goals. You must make this clear or you will be disappointed when he or she doesn't meet your expectations.

5. Keep the Excitement Alive

When you're working on a particular goal for a lengthy period there will, without doubt, be times when you will hit a 'wall', and this will dent your enthusiasm somewhat. You are not alone. Everyone has to navigate his or her way through the jungle, and occasionally we will get smacked in the face by a thorny branch. We all carry the scars to prove this. Each time this happens it can deplete your energy, leaving you feeling deflated and disappointed. You *will* hit blocks, so get used to it, but do not let them dilute your excitement or fervour. You must keep your dream alive, no matter what!

When you have a bad day and feel your excitement dwindling, do something that reconnects you with your original dream. When I am working towards a particular goal I make sure I visualize the final outcome every day, as this ensures that my focus is where it needs to be and away from any setbacks or obstacles. If you allow yourself to be affected by setbacks it will snuff out your enthusiasm, which perpetually leads you to procrastinate and take no further action. Think of ways to keep your excitement alive.

One client, when she felt she was moving off-base, would visit her local car dealership and sit in the car she intended to buy herself when she'd achieved her goals. Simple, but it made the world of difference to her mindset. She told me that she would always come away with a renewed sense of vigour and drive.

Another client created a 'vision board' full of magazine pictures that represented the life she would be living once she had achieved her goals. She used colourful images of beautiful landscapes, her ideal home and garden, and a picture of a happy family. She made her vision board as emotive as she possibly could so that every time she looked at it she felt joyful and reconnected to her goals. It reminded her why she set them in the first place.

When you feel your excitement deteriorating, ask yourself: what can I do immediately to lift my mood?

(Examples might be go for a walk, put on my favourite music or contact my coaching buddy.)

6. Don't Tell the World

Remember, when you start making big changes to your life, people start to notice – and most of them don't like it. This is because it highlights their own inability to transform their own lives. Don't be upset by this; it is human nature. We compare ourselves to others, and this is always going to be futile. This is why it is imperative to have a coaching buddy or a support network to call on, someone who can share your dreams with you so you don't feel you have to tell every Tom, Dick and Harry about them to get the support you need. And if you have had a bad day, this way you don't whinge at everyone. Share your frustration with your coaching buddy, your support network or your Inner Guide. Keep your dreams to yourself, and don't tell the world. Other people will only add their 'two-penn'orth' and, in the process steal a little bit of your positive energy.

> *There is nothing better than accomplishing a goal completely and then announcing it to the world – it's an awesome feeling!*

Perhaps it will help to think of it as being in the early stages of your first pregnancy and keeping it 'hush-hush' until you've reached the safe zone of 12 weeks. Think how wonderful it is to walk around knowing you have such a special secret. It feels incredible! There is something magical about keeping your intentions and dreams to yourself, and then announcing them when you're absolutely ready.

CLEARING OUT THE RUBBISH

Before we start getting into action I want you to get your house in order. How can you expect to be focused if your physical environment is filled with clutter? As the saying goes, 'A clear house equals a clear mind.' If you're consistently looking at unfinished DIY projects or have a cascade of crumpled clothes fall on your head each time you open the wardrobe door, it's only going to add to your stress levels and take your attention away from where it needs to be. Make an inventory of your house or office and list all the jobs that you've been putting off for months, or even years. Are there unused clothes in the spare room? Are there piles of old DVDs, books, paperwork, old letters and bills cluttering up your shelves or cupboards? If so it's time to clear them out, once and for all. Remember, this is the start of your new life, so what better time to tackle it? You never know, you might even raise some cash to help fund your goals.

Exercise

Make a list of ten niggly jobs you need to do and put the list on the fridge door! Spend the weekend or a few evenings sorting these jobs out, once and for all. Get some help if you need to, but get them done.

TIME TO GET INTO ACTION!

Before you do anything else I want you to do one of the following:

- Buy a diary

- Create a coaching folder

- Buy a journal.

I want you to have a book to keep all your ideas, strategies and actions in one place. The last things you need are scraps of paper all over your house. It's time to get organized! If you've never been the organized type, now is the time to start. Take a trip to your local stationer's and buy all the equipment you think you're going to need. It doesn't have to be expensive; a cardboard folder will keep everything in one place. Looking at each of your goals in turn, write a list of potential contacts or supports that you have at your fingertips. Perhaps friends, an old boss, good books, workshops, seminars, local resources such as your library, and so on. List anyone and anything that will help you bring about your goals.

Recruit Your Coaching Buddy

Make a list of five potential coaching buddies. Once you have done this, write down three advantages and three disadvantages for each person. Evaluate and make your final decision as to who is the best person for the job.

Your very first action is to phone your selected coaching buddy and advise them about your plans. Share your goals, tell your buddy about this book and ask whether he or she is prepared and committed to help you on your passage to your new life. If he or she agrees, suggest that you get together for a coffee so you can make a start.

Write the name of your chosen coaching buddy here:

_____

The date of your first meeting is:

_____

Create Your Strategies

It's time to create your strategy for each goal. Use a blank piece of paper and brainstorm all the major areas you think you'll need to cover in order to reach each of your goals. Don't worry about their order at this stage: just list everything that comes to mind. You're looking for between three and eight strategies for each of your goals. If you find you have a list of nine or more, refine and amalgamate your list until you have no more than eight.

Once you have your strategies, first put them into a logical order and then write down your final list. This is the plan you will be following from now until you achieve your goals.

Start Creating Your Actions

Unlike strategies, you simply cannot map out every action you're going to take in advance. It's impossible. Your actions must remain fluid, as they will change on an almost daily basis. As new ideas and insight flow into your consciousness, your actions will inevitably alter; this is exactly as it should be. To begin setting your actions, you need to take your first strategy for each goal and think of approximately four or five smaller steps which you can take to kick-start your goals in the right direction.

Write down your first five actions for each of your three goals.

Well done! You're off the starting blocks. It's important that you now ensure you take the time to complete each and every action/step. No procrastinating, as this will just slow things down. If you find yourself postponing an action, ask yourself why. What limiting belief is sabotaging your success?

Imagine how wonderful you'll feel when you get to the end of the week having achieved all 15 actions – fantastic, I promise. But it doesn't end there! Now you've got the ball rolling, it is essential that you sit down at the same time every week and re-evaluate each of your actions, and then set brand new ones to take your goal forwards to the next stage. This is how the process must work if you want to succeed.

Be sure to recognize your achievements and give yourself a good old pat on the back.

How Will You Celebrate Your Successes?

As you travel along the path of success, it's important that you praise yourself for all your achievements: because if you don't, no one else will. Write down every success that you have achieved – from making a simple phone call to securing a new contract. Remember, when you do this you are creating solid evidence that will help you to form a healthy mindset which will ensure you make it to the finishing line. Evidence list aside, I also recommend that every time you complete each strategy you find a way of celebrating your accomplishments, either on your own, with family or with your coaching buddy.

Here are some suggestions:

• Buy yourself a treat, maybe a new book or a new handbag.

• Open a bottle of bubbly.

• Pamper yourself: have a massage or your favourite beauty treatment.

• Go out to your favourite café or restaurant for something to eat.

• Do something you've always wanted to, such as ice-skating or a singing lesson, parachuting, hot air ballooning, going on an assault course or having a spa weekend away.

List ten ways you will celebrate your successes.

Your Self-belief

What do you need to believe so that each of your goals becomes reality? Your beliefs play a huge part in achieving or failing to achieve your goals. If you do not adopt the right mindset, you will fall short and your journey will be fraught.

For each of your three goals, write down (in the present tense) three new beliefs that you must start working on in order for you to change your mindset and, ultimately, triumph. For example, your new belief might be 'I am full of creative ideas,' 'I am strong and can do anything I set my mind to' or, 'Every day new opportunities are flowing into my life.'

It's not enough for your beliefs just to be written in your notebook, diary, journal or whatever method you're using. You need to see your new beliefs every single day. Write down each new belief on a Post-it® note three or four times and stick the notes around the house. The bathroom mirror is always a good place, or how about the inside of your wardrobe door, your car dashboard, your kitchen cupboards or computer? Make sure you affirm these new beliefs as often as you can.

Excitement Boosters

It's vital to keep your excitement alive. It will naturally ebb and flow, but you need to keep the overall passion burning. Don't allow the flame to go out.

List five ways you intend to keep your excitement alive, from creating a vision board to mixing with successful people or visiting a particular place.

YOUR DAILY WORKOUT

This book is about finding a whole new way of living, and if you truly want to achieve your goals you are going to have to start doing things differently. If you continue to live your life as you have always done, you will keep getting the same results. It's as simple as that. I have given you all the tools you need to help you generate the life you want to lead, but the buck stops here. It's over to you now. If you want to succeed, it's time to change, once and for all. I want you to create a daily mental workout that will ensure you cannot fail. Here's an example:

- 7 a.m. Visualize my day in advance, seeing everything going the way I want.

- 7.30 a.m. While in shower, repeat positive affirmations ten times each.

- 8.30 a.m. While driving or on the bus, listen to an inspirational audio tape.

- 12.30 p.m. Spend lunch hour working on actions/ steps.

- 5 p.m. While driving home or on the bus, listen to an inspirational audio tape.

- 5.30 p.m. Continue working on actions/steps.

- 6.30 p.m. Spend 20 minutes meditating and visualizing future.

- 11 p.m. Before going to sleep, repeat affirmations one final time, or maybe listen to a self-hypnosis audio tape.

Start right now!
What are you waiting for?

YOUR HOMEPLAY THIS WEEK

1. Make a habit of stepping out of your comfort zone: do one thing per day that scares the hell out of you.

2. Clear out the rubbish in your home or office.

3. Buy a coaching diary or folder.

4. Recruit your coaching buddy and set a date for your first meeting.

5. Work out the strategy for each of your goals.

6. Set your first set of actions.

7. Write down what you need to believe about yourself in order to achieve your goals.

8. Commit to a daily workout. Make a list of the new habits/rituals you want to incorporate into your life and start doing them!

CHAPTER 8

Facing Your Fears

So what happens when you've created your magnificent life-changing goals, you've mapped out your strategies and you've even signed up your coaching buddy, and you find yourself hiding in a cupboard, paralysed by fear and unable to peek outside? What do you do then?

In this final chapter I will show you how to face your fears head-on and how to bounce back with vigour and determination.

Let's get one thing clear: everyone has fears, some small and some big. Some of us fear getting it wrong, looking like an idiot, changing jobs, losing our relationship, getting old, public speaking, swimming or even being a bad parent. We all have something we fear at some level. It's human nature. We are programmed to be fearful of the unknown.

In this day and age we are conditioned to fear everything, from a spider on the wall to the world at large. We fear change, we fear beginnings, we fear endings, we fear living and we even fear dying. Fear may be so all-consuming, immense and debilitating that it keeps you stuck within your comfort zone for decades without ever moving forwards. The more time that passes, the worse the fear gets. You end up living your life in limbo, feeling disappointed, prodded and let down by life. Life in the shadow of fear is a horrible place to reside.

You must not let fear rob you of the opportunity to succeed and grow in life. Yet I often tell my clients that if they are not fearful they are not progressing or growing. Fear is just a clear sign that we've reached the edge of our comfort zone. The question is: 'Will you jump off into the unknown or run back?'

> *What people don't realize is that fear is a normal part of life, and it is essential if you want to live up to your true potential.*

Fear is encapsulated within the very essence of goal-setting. When you venture into new territory, you will come face to face with your own personal demons. The key is not to run as fast as you can in the opposite direction, but to face fear head-on – believe me, it's never as bad as you think it's going to be.

I almost allowed fear to sabotage my dreams when I signed up to my life-coach training programme. It had been a long time since I'd done any type of formal training and I was petrified at the thought of doing assignments and taking exams. Would I be able to keep up? Would I like the people I was training with? What would happen if I didn't pass? What if I realized coaching wasn't my dream after all? I remember my train pulling into London's Euston Station on a frosty cold January morning. It was the first day of my training programme. As I looked around the carriage I wondered what everyone else was doing in London: were they there to work, to see family, to shop? As I stood up and approached the train door I could feel the palms of my hands become more and more sweaty. I gripped the handle of my little green weekend bag for extra comfort, trying to imagine it was my husband's hand instead. It didn't work. What was I doing?! It was the first time I had been to London alone and I could feel the panic start to take hold of my body. My chest tightened and my breathing became shallow. I remember thinking that maybe I could just spend the weekend shopping instead. Who would know?

As I stepped off the train, I joined the frenzied commuters all trying to make their way to the exit. Even with hundreds of people walking to my left and right, I had never felt quite so lonely. I could have cried. It would have been so easy to have jumped on the next train home and forgotten all about my dreams of starting a new career. When I got out of the station, the cold winter sunshine hit my colourless face and somewhere deep inside I heard the gentle voice of my Inner Guide saying... 'You can do this, Louise,' and I immediately felt better. I flagged down a black cab (I wasn't going attempt the Tube, oh no) and made my way to the venue. As the morning progressed, my fear slowly subsided. I met some of the most amazing people that weekend, and the memory of the experience stays firmly locked within my mind as one of the major achievements in my career thus far.

Remember, each time you face a fear your comfort zone expands and, in turn, so does your life.

When we feel an emotion that is uncomfortable, such as fear, many of us tend to run away or push it aside, often by distracting ourselves with food, TV, the internet and so on, or simply by swallowing the feeling and continuing to live our lives in the shadow of fear. When you find that nothing seems to ease your apprehension, embrace it. It's OK to be fearful, it's a natural part of life, it means you're growing; it means that you've made a decision to move forwards. Experience the fear and let it move through your body. Remember, it's never as bad as you think it's going to be!

Every successful person has felt fear on his or her journey to a better life. It's part of life and unavoidable, so you need to get used to it. Often we do things to avoid having to deal with the fear we're facing. Here are some common signs to look out for:

- Rather than take a specific action, you find yourself looking for distractions or new projects: you start clearing out cupboards you haven't touched for ten years, or redecorating your bedroom.

- You start phoning every friend in your phonebook, or lose yourself in social networking.

- You start watching TV or listening to the radio more.

- You find yourself eating more.

- You feel apathetic and tired.

- You get cross when anyone asks how you are getting on with your goals.

- You find yourself offering to take the dog for a walk, even though it's not your job.

- You volunteer to stay late at work or work the weekend.

- You get involved in other people's crises.

- You find yourself being very negative and pessimistic.

- You avoid all calls from your coaching buddy!

GET COMFORTABLE WITH FAILURE

If you are going to make it to the finishing line, you have to be comfortable with the idea of failing. In most cases it's not the actual failing that's terrifying, it's the fear of failing that really paralyses people. You must understand that fear is just an emotion. Feelings are all the same, whether you're happy, sad, angry or frightened. They are only emotions and not something from outside of you. Feelings are derived from the thoughts you hold and the images that you play out in your mind, so in order to change your feelings it makes sense that you change the thoughts and images in your head. When you feel scared, it's normally because you have allowed your Inner Critic to consume your mind with negative thoughts! Whenever your Inner Critic has an opportunity to pounce on you and prove that your original negative beliefs were true, it will do. It will say, 'When are you going to stop kidding yourself and get back to your "real" life?' or 'Stop fooling yourself, you know you'll never succeed.' Your Inner Critic will sabotage your success at every opportunity if you let it.

When you find yourself consumed by the harmful voice of your Inner Critic and totally rooted to the spot with terror, it's a clear sign that it's time to tune in to your Inner Guide. Change the pictures in your mind, or the thoughts in your head, to something more positive. It's up to you to take control. If your mind is powerful enough to make you feel down, conversely it is also powerful enough to make you feel good; it's just a state of mind. Remember, all emotions are the same; we decide which are good or bad.

Life is too short to be afraid. You need to cultivate the mindset of the truly successful. They, too, feel fear, but they have learned how to turn their trepidation to their advantage and use fear to propel them forwards. Let others plod through life; it's time to get serious about living the life you really want.

IT'S ONLY FEEDBACK!

One vital piece of advice I received when starting my journey was that failure is simply feedback. Think about it for a second: failing is just feedback! It doesn't mean it's the end of the road, or that it's time to give up. It's a pointer to prompt you to change direction. This critical bit of information helped me to turn the concept of failure completely on its head. Look at it like this: when something goes wrong, if you don't get the deal you were banking on, or if someone turns you down for a date you were looking forwards to, instead of seeing it as a failure or the end of the story, see it as feedback from the universe or your Inner Guide telling you to try a different route. When something in my own life doesn't go according to plan, rather than beating myself up for days on end and allowing myself to become downhearted, I think, 'OK, that obviously wasn't the best path to follow; there must be something better on the horizon.' I then let go of all judgement and wait for fresh inspiration to flow into my consciousness. And, amazingly, it always does, and the new ideas are always far better.

At one point I hit a major roadblock and the feeling of failure nearly sabotaged a lifelong dream. What seemed like complete failure at the time turned out to be a wonderful blessing in disguise. I had started my new life-coaching business while I was still in full-time employment. Needless to say, it was hard work working from 9 to 5 and then having to come home and start my second job. But at the time it was necessary as, of course, it is for most people when they are starting out. I thought I was superwoman and could do it all: hold down a job, be a good mother, run a home and, on top of all these, start a new business. Things were fine for a time but it wasn't going to be sustainable, even though I thought it was. Something had to give. On top of all that, I decided it would be a great idea to get pregnant!

Yes, I know. I must have been living in 'la-la land'. But I had what I thought was a perfectly timed 'Grand

Plan'. I would have the baby, go on maternity leave and enjoy the time with my new baby while growing my new life-coaching practice. After my maternity leave (when I had lots of new clients in the bag), I would inform my employer I wouldn't be returning to work, giving me the perfect lifestyle that I was desperately seeking. What a great opportunity to build my business without having to take any risks at all! I had it all mapped out. What I failed to do at the time was listen to my Inner Guide. I ignored all guidance or gut feeling I had and simply followed my logic, and took what I thought would be the best and easiest route. And because life was so hectic at the time, I rarely found a moment for meditation or visualizing. I had completely lost my spiritual connection.

This was to be futile. Three months into my pregnancy I lost my baby unexpectedly and, as you can imagine, it was a horrible shock. Not only did I lose my baby, I almost lost my own life as well as I suffered a huge haemorrhage and had to be rushed into hospital. Not a pleasant experience, I can tell you. The weeks that followed were spent in bed wallowing in self-pity. I had failed. My Grand Plan had failed and I felt as if my world had collapsed around me.

I didn't know which way to turn. I tried to work out why it had happened, but I just felt as if I had a dense fog clouding my vision. I had lost my clarity. I had lost direction. It wasn't until a few months later that the fog finally lifted and it all became very clear indeed.

Going through such a traumatic experience forced me to re-evaluate my life. It helped me to make some huge life-changing decisions. Subsequently I was able to see what a fool I had been, allowing myself to take on so much pressure. Shortly after this I handed in my notice and went self-employed. I'm sure I wouldn't have made this decision without having gone through my so-called 'failure'. The blessings that have come out of this have been incredible. A year or so on, after spending lots of quality time growing my new life-coaching practice, I fell pregnant again and went on to have a healthy baby boy.

You may or may not experience such traumas on your journey (I certainly hope not!). But when things go wrong, we need to listen – it's vital feedback. I had plenty of feedback along the way, I just ignored it. I thought I knew best and stopped listening to my Inner Guide. Remember, feedback comes in lots of different ways. It may be a missed train, a cancelled meeting or a rejection of some kind.

Failure is simply feedback and an opportunity to step back and look at your situation with fresh eyes. When you can do this you'll see the real truth of your situation.

DEALING WITH KNOCK-BACKS

There will be knock-backs from time to time. There will be times when you think to yourself 'I can't do this any more!' I haven't met anyone who hasn't had to deal with some kind of obstacle on the way to the finishing line. The key is how you deal with knock-backs. The truly successful pick themselves up, dust themselves down and carry on. However, most of us don't do this and we use knock-backs as 'proof' that our original negative belief ('I can't do this') was right all along. We use it as evidence that we were deluding ourselves, and then we woefully retreat back into our comfort zone. The more we do this, the stronger becomes the belief that we are incapable of making changes to our lives. Eventually we don't even try to attempt anything new because we expect to fall flat on our face. And because we *expect* to fall short, we invariably do!

Below are two examples of remarkable human beings who, when faced with huge setbacks, decided *not* to call it a day. Instead they laughed in the face of adversity and went on to achieve remarkable things.

At the age of just 13, Bethany Hamilton was an aspiring surfing star. On the morning of 31 October 2003, Bethany and a few friends went out surfing as they usually did:

> *I was lying on my board, parallel to the waves. One of my arms was lying in the water and the other was just holding the board. Then the shark just came up and attacked me, and it kind of pulled me back and forth. It was only, like, two or three seconds, so it was really quick.*

Bethany lost her entire left arm. Did she let this major knock-back stop her? No. Within six months she was surfing again, and winning.

Ray Kroc founded McDonald's at the age of 52, when he realized that people didn't want to dine in any more, but would eat 'on the run' instead. At the time Ray Kroc had diabetes and had had to have his gallbladder and most of his thyroid gland removed. But he had a clear conviction that the best was ahead of him!

Stephen Hawking was diagnosed with motor neurone disease aged just 21, and doctors said he would not survive more than three years. Over a short period of time he lost the use of his arms, legs and voice, and was almost completely paralysed. But this was not the end to his journey. As we all know, Professor Hawking is one of the world's most famous scientists. He has 12 honorary degrees, was awarded the CBE in 1982 and was made a Companion of Honour in 1989. He is the recipient of many awards, medals and prizes and is a Fellow of The Royal Society and a Member of the US National Academy of Sciences. If these remarkable people can pick themselves up and carry on, so can you. Yes, you will be disappointed when you are rejected, turned down or refused, but remember: it's only feedback and an opportunity to consider taking a different direction. See it for the blessing it really is.

> As the great Greek philosopher Epictetus once said, 'It's not what happens to you, but how you react to it that matters.'

There have been lots of roadblocks on my journey, but there have also been many wonderful blessings that wouldn't have come about if it weren't for these so-called obstructions. Sometimes I did find it hard to scrape my flattened ego off the floor and start again, but I did it. It didn't feel great, but I was on a huge learning curve and I made sure I never repeated my mistakes. When I work with clients, part of my job is to support them when they feel as if they have been hit by a truck and are left feeling completely bewildered. This is why it's so important to have a coaching buddy to give you the support you need when things go wrong. It can make all the difference.

When we don't have support it's easy to pretend we've done all that we can and just give up. The key is to pick yourself up as quickly as possible and continue on your way: when you fall off your horse, you should get straight back on again. Do not linger, as this will only make things appear worse. Find a way that makes you feel better. We'll look at how to do this shortly.

So let me ask you:

> *How you will choose to respond to the challenges before you? Will you give up, or will you be a fighter and forge on?*

DON'T TAKE 'NO' FOR AN ANSWER!

One thing I have become fascinated with over recent years is what makes some individuals more successful than others. Why do some people achieve awesome things? What do they do differently from other people? Of course a lot has to do with adopting the right mindset, but another important ingredient to being successful is persistence. Tenacity plays a huge role in whether or not you are going to achieve your goals.

I met a multi-millionaire around the time I was about to leave my job to go self-employed. By chance

I happened to be sitting in his office, along with a friend. I'd never met a multi-millionaire before and I was rather curious. As I looked around the office all I could see was evidence of this man's achievements. There were placards on the walls displaying awards that he'd won, and there were pictures of him mingling with the world's rich and famous, not to mention a glass-topped table and the biggest widescreen TV I'd ever seen mounted on the far wall. It was another world, and I wanted to know how he'd created it. I wanted to know what made this man so successful?

As we sat talking I had an impulse to ask him what his secret was. I knew that once I'd walked out of his office I wouldn't get the opportunity again. I waited for a break in the conversation and, ignoring my pounding heart and the screams of my Inner Critic, asked, 'You're obviously a very successful man, and I'm just about to set up my own company. Would you mind me asking, what is the secret to your success?' My friend looked at me in horror. We were here to discuss a contract we were working on at the time, and I had dared to bring my personal life into the conversation. Obviously she thought I'd lost the plot and was about to get both of us fired.

He turned to me with a twinkle in his eyes. I knew what he was thinking. I'd never been the quiet type and had always firmly believed (and still do) that if you don't ask, you don't get! Giving me a warm smile he said, very calmly, 'Above all: don't give up. Don't be scared to go where you think others have already been before you. BE PERSISTENT until you get to where you want to be.' He smiled again and I knew without doubt that he respected my nerve for asking the question.

I decided at that point that 'persistence' was to become my new mantra.

There have been many occasions when I have put this advice to good use. When I started my new business, like so many others I had little money for advertising. I specifically recall sitting at my dining table one wet and dreary Sunday afternoon trying to brainstorm ways to attract new customers. Then the brainwave struck. I knew from past experience that newspapers and magazines were always looking for interesting stories to fill their pages. If I could get a regular column, or even a one-off feature, people would read it and I could start to get my message out. Free advertising! So I sat down that evening and wrote my very first article. Then came the hard bit: on the Monday morning I started researching relevant magazines, both locally and regionally, and started to email my article to them. I sent 25 emails that day, and no one responded. No, that's a lie: I had three responses, all saying, 'Thank you, but no thank you.' I felt flat as a pancake. At this point most people would have given up, convincing themselves that they had tried very hard but it wasn't going to work. But when you hit this point you should see your so-called setback as vital feedback – and try a different route instead. And that is what I did. I knew if I could get my face into some magazines, clients would start flowing in. So the next day, after spending all morning procrastinating, drinking endless cups of tea and making unnecessary calls to friends, I finally plucked up the courage to contact some of the editors I had emailed the previous day. Much to my surprise they were very pleasant and said they would keep my details on file. I didn't get a 'yes' that day, but I moved the parameters of my comfort zone a little and it felt good. Over the months that followed I made a point of emailing these editors each and every time I wrote a new article and, within six months, I had regular features in five magazines. What a result! If I hadn't been persistent and had given up at the first hurdle, I wouldn't have been encouraged to write for bigger magazines and eventually write this book!

The moral of this story is: do not take 'No' for an answer! Change direction and find another way.

LEARN FROM THE BEST

I think if we were to sit down with an entrepreneur or an Olympic gold medallist, they would all say that their journey to a better life was not easy, or painless. These individuals achieve amazing things by refusing to be put off. They have a clear vision of where they are going and let nothing deter them. The rags-to-riches story of J. K. Rowling is a fascinating one. The idea for Harry Potter was first born while she was stuck on a delayed train from Manchester to London. J. K. Rowling started working on her book, but was then cast into the role of single mother; her life altered and she moved to Scotland to be near her sister and found herself surviving on benefits while she looked for teaching work. But J. K. Rowling continued to pursue her dream of writing. Eventually she finished her manuscript, found an agent at the second attempt and sent it off to several publishers, only for it to be rejected. But she didn't see this as the end of the road; she simply tried again and again. Eventually, after a year of trying, a publisher agreed to take on her work.

As we all know, when *Harry Potter and the Philosopher's Stone* was published in 1997 it was an instant success with both children and adults. J. K. Rowling's personal story is an astonishing reversal of fortune: from struggling single parent to the most successful author on the planet.

Another inspiring story is that of Jim Carrey. Jim had to drop out of high school to take a job as a janitor, working in a factory alongside other members of his family. But Jim had a passion for comedy and had a clear picture of what he wanted from life. He actually wrote himself a $10 million cheque as a reminder of his inevitable future success. After working on the comedy circuit for many years he landed a part in the TV series *In Living Color*. After this Jim moved on to film roles. His hits have included *Ace Ventura*, *The Mask* and *Dumb and Dumber*, to name but a few, and Jim Carrey is now one of the highest-paid actors in Hollywood.

Did you know that it took James Dyson 5,127 prototypes, 14 years of debt and multiple lawsuits to create the top-selling upright vacuum cleaner? Or that it took Thomas Edison over 3,000 attempts to create the lightbulb? When he was asked about the failures he said, 'I didn't fail 3,000 times; I found 3,000 ways how not to create a lightbulb.' What a great mindset! What I'm trying to demonstrate is that the vast majority of 'overnight' successes really took a lot longer; it's just that we don't usually get to know the full story. Just like us, people who have succeeded in achieving their goals have had to work hard, make difficult decisions and have undoubtedly come up against blockages that have altered the course of their path.

We have to understand that failure is just part of life when achieving big goals. If you remain steadfast to your original vision – while also being open to adjusting the path that gets you there – you will succeed. Turn yourself into someone who is totally solution-focused. As soon as obstacles present themselves, make a commitment to yourself to find a better way, because when you do this you will be shown a new way. I promise.

SELF-SABOTAGE

One thing I want you to become aware of, especially now that you're in the process of setting up your weekly action steps, is your unique self-sabotaging style. By 'self-sabotage' I mean subconscious behaviours, or habits, that you perform which slow down your progress or stop you moving forwards altogether.

Your unique self-sabotaging style is always derived from your innermost fears of failure. We all have a self-sabotaging style, and some of us have more than one. They are familiar, long-standing behaviours that you put in place many moons ago as a safety mechanism.

Just as you need to be aware of your Inner Critic, you need to be alert to self-sabotage. Once you are aware of your own self-sabotaging behaviours, you will be able to see them for what they really are and quickly move on, instead of letting them hold you back.

Remember, awareness is the key.

I realized my own self-sabotaging style early on, and was surprised at the harmful impact I allowed it to have on my life. My style was procrastination. As always I would form my weekly 'to do' list – but what I found myself doing was putting the easiest jobs at the top of my list and the more challenging jobs at the bottom. This invariably meant I would never get round to my more difficult tasks. Of course it felt great every time I crossed yet another small action off my list, but I was just kidding myself, as none of the bigger, more challenging actions was ever reached. I found myself rewriting these more difficult items on my 'to do' list week after week.

Basically, if anything was outside my comfort zone I would find something that would distract me from having to take action. I'd eat; I'd call my mum for a chat. I'd pop to the shops or decide it was a good time to reorganize my kitchen cupboards. I'd be delighted if the phone rang, as this was the ultimate distraction and the perfect excuse to not take action. I'd then realize, 'Oh, dear it's 5 p.m. I'll have to do it tomorrow.' And the story repeated itself until I woke up and brought my self-sabotaging style to light and finally put an end to it. I say 'put an end to it', but, just like your Inner Critic, it will pop up when you least expect it. Even now I find myself falling into the procrastination trap and I have to pull myself out quickly before it takes hold. On many occasions while writing this book I'd find myself delaying action, especially when I found a particular section difficult or more challenging to write. I would tell myself I needed another chocolate biscuit, anything that would delay action and extinguish my fear of failure. It's safer not to take action as this means you'll never have to deal with rejection. But this means you live your life in limbo, never really moving forwards.

Other people have quite different styles of sabotage. Some individuals are perfectionists. They'll fixate on one route and insist that's the only way. They'll perform whatever it is they are working on at least a hundred times before they're happy and satisfied with it. It has to be faultless or they don't take any action whatsoever. This means things rarely get finished; they always have endless lists of unfinished tasks, from DIY to personal projects.

Much like procrastination, perfectionism has its own drawbacks and, if you let it, it will interfere with your goals.

When I work with my clients over a period of time I start to notice their self-sabotaging styles. Of course, no one really likes to be told about their flaws, but it's important to be aware of them if you want to achieve big things in life. Below I have listed what are (in my experience) the top six self-sabotaging styles:

1. Procrastination: we delay action, insisting other things must take precedence before goals can be progressed.

2. Perfectionism: we keep re-doing something because it must be perfect, but in doing so we never seem to move any closer to our goals.

3. Dreaming: blissfully spending our time dreaming about how wonderful life will be when we achieve our goals. We create wonderful plans, lists and vision boards, but never take any real action.

4. Laziness: we expect everyone around us to take action for us, and won't take any action ourselves.

5. Blaming others: we won't take responsibility and blame everyone else for our past failures or inaction.

6. Being an airhead: being disorganized and running around, never seeming to make progress. Airheads never move any closer to their goals because they're always too busy dealing with one crisis or another.

Exercise

Answer the following questions.

- *How do you best sabotage yourself?*

- *What kind of things do you do when you are in this style?*

- *How does this affect your progress?*

So, what's the solution? Well, unfortunately, there isn't a magic pill that will miraculously cure you of your self-sabotaging. Just as with your Inner Guide and Inner Critic, you simply need to become aware of it. Once you are conscious of your preferred self-sabotaging style, you can change your behaviour to something more advantageous. Notice when you fall into your sabotaging style and do the opposite to what you'd normally do. Again, this is why it pays to have a coaching buddy, as others will notice your self-sabotaging style far better than you will yourself. When I find myself procrastinating around a certain action, I don't chastise myself, I simply laugh at myself instead and say, 'Caught you!' We're great at kidding ourselves that we're making headway even though we're just going round and round in circles, going nowhere fast. Be aware!

RE-ADDRESS YOUR BELIEFS

When you find it impossible to get out of the habit of sabotaging yourself, it's time to re-address your beliefs once again. When a long-standing belief is deep-rooted, your Inner Critic will do its utmost to keep you tied to it, no matter what. If you find this is the case, it's time to look again at your limiting beliefs and start practising the exercises we've already spoken about in previous chapters. When we sabotage ourselves it's because we are still running an old negative belief, and the best way to change an old belief is to feel the fear and carry out the action we're terrified of doing. When we do this we are not only expanding our comfort zone, we are also programming our mind with a 'can do' attitude. When I ask clients what is getting in the way of them moving forwards, many of them recall times in their lives when they have failed. This is a clear sign that some old programming is still running. Thinking about past failures is a sure-fire way to shoot yourself in the foot, and is certainly not helpful! This is why it is essential to address your negative beliefs and start doing something about them.

BOUNCING BACK FROM ADVERSITY

Having worked with hundreds of people who have made enormous life changes, and having made some extensive changes to my own life, I have come to realize that sometimes we all need time to take stock of where we are before we can find the energy to move on. And there is absolutely nothing wrong with this, as long as we don't stay still for too long!

There have been days when I have experienced a particular setback which has left me feeling flummoxed, and I've decided that the best thing to do is to shut my laptop, put on my pyjamas and watch my favourite film.

> *Remember, you cannot make a silk purse from a sow's ear: taking action from a negative space will always be futile.*

People can smell fear and they feel your anxiety! When you feel pessimistic it is better to take no action at all than to take action derived from fear or panic. Obviously the children still need to be picked up from school or the food needs to be bought. I'm not talking about this kind of inaction. I'm talking about 'inspired' action. When we're fearful, apathetic or anxious it's never advisable to take new actions because the results won't be beneficial, thus adding to our plight. Always, always, wait until you feel strong again before you take your next step, that way you know the results will be in line with what you want. Remember how the Law of Attraction works.

TAKING TIME OUT

When you feel as if you're at the edge of a 100-foot drop and about to be pushed over the edge, or when your Inner Critic has completely saturated every good thought in your head, it's a clear sign to take some time out. Don't feel bad about this. We all need time out occasionally; it doesn't mean you're weak or on the road to ruin. It just means you need a little time to refill your energy tank. Just like your car, you, too, cannot function if your energy tank is running dry. It's important to notice when this happens. So many of us fail to recognize the 'red light' in front of our eyes and end up causing ourselves enormous turmoil.

Here are some clear signs that you're in need of some time out:

- You don't seem to have time to eat or, worse still, go to the loo.

- You realize you haven't seen your wife or kids all week.

- You are consistently working till 10 p.m. every night.

- You're checking your emails every five minutes.

- You feel anxious and panicky all the time.

- You have no time to look after yourself or pursue your hobbies.

- You grab unhealthy snacks instead of preparing nutritious meals.

- You're using alcohol or cigarettes to relax you.

- You can't sleep because your head is spinning.

- You don't want to get out of bed in the morning.

- You look tired and worn out.

- You're always ill.

When you find you're experiencing any of the above, be kind to yourself, stop what you are doing and take some much-needed time out, because if you don't you'll miss some vital piece of the jigsaw and will inevitably be thrown off-course. This is where I went wrong just before I had my miscarriage. I was experiencing all of the above signs: I was working all hours; I was obsessed, and I mean totally obsessed, with checking my website stats and emails; and the worst of it was I saw so little of my daughter I felt like I had custody of her for only one or two hours a week!

But I couldn't see any of this at the time. Others around me could, but I simply wouldn't listen. The universe was desperately trying to steer me away from impact, but I couldn't hear the messages my Inner Guide was giving me and eventually it all ended in tears. I will never let this happen to me again. I have learned my lesson. So, please, take heed and listen to your body and inner spirit because, when we are tuned in, we will be given all the directions we need to take our goals forwards.

Now, when I say 'time out' I'm not talking about taking a sabbatical. I'm not suggesting you park your goals for a few months until you feel ready to carry on. Oh, no! I'm talking about a day, a few days – a week at most, just enough time to restore your energy levels. Sometimes just an early night, a good long walk or having a fun day out can make the world of difference.

Have you ever noticed when you're away from your office, desk, computer or whatever, that ideas start to flow? You are inspired with new thoughts, things that you simply couldn't think previously? It really does pay to take time out.

Here are some examples of things you can do while talking time out:

- Spend the day in your comfy clothes or pyjamas and do nothing!

- Go for a long walk, alone or with your family.

- Spend time with Nature, smell the roses; literally, appreciate life!

- Get your hands dirty in the garden.

- Spend the day with the kids doing off-the-wall things; give them 100 per cent attention!

- Help out someone in need: a friend, a neighbour or family member; take your focus off yourself.

- Clear out your cupboards or garage.

- Repaint a room in your house in a new colour.

- Think about ways you can simplify your life, such as hiring a cleaner, hiring an accountant, doing your grocery shopping online and so on.

- Read a good book or watch a DVD.

- Go away for the weekend.

LOWER YOUR SIGHTS

When you're feeling let down, disappointed or disillusioned, a great remedy is to lower your sights somewhat. I don't mean revamp your entire goal and downscale it completely. What I'm suggesting is taking the smallest step you possibly can to move your goal forwards until you feel strong again. If you're overwhelmed, rather than letting your fear grind you to a halt entirely, take the tiniest step you can think of. Just taking one tiny step will feel a lot better than taking no action at all.

For example, if you have been procrastinating for several days over making an important call to someone, break the action down. Perhaps send an email beforehand, or leave a message asking them to call you. It doesn't matter how small your action, as long as you're moving forwards and not remaining motionless. When my clients fall into the procrastination trap, I ask them, 'How can you change your action to make it seem less scary?' Sometimes we can be a little too ambitious with our actions because we're excited and keen to push ahead. There is nothing wrong with this, but, remember, high achievers take lots of little steps, not huge leaps or hurdles. Taking small steps or actions is without doubt the best route to achieving any goal. It's a bit like trying to lose weight. We all know that the most sensible way of shedding the pounds is by losing the weight slowly, maybe one or two pounds a week. When you lose too much too soon you invariably end up putting it all back on again, and hence the yo-yo syndrome is born. If you're stuck, break your goal down into the smallest step you can possibly take – and then take it!

You'll not only get the wheels in motion again, you'll also feel fantastic in the process.

FOCUS ON PAST SUCCESSES

We discussed, in Chapter 3, how keeping a list of evidence is a great way of re-programming your mind for success.

This evidence list will also come into its own when you find yourself unable to move. There is something very uplifting about looking back at your past successes. It's a superb way of helping you to get motivated and regain your gusto. It offers hard, undeniable proof that you are triumphant and able to accomplish remarkable things. So when you need a boost, get out your evidence list, have yourself a coffee and a biscuit (or even two!) and celebrate your past successes. Often my clients come to their session telling me they've had a really unproductive week and have not made much progress. In reality, this is not often the whole truth. When I probe a little further it usually turns out that they've made excellent headway but there have been one or two particular actions they didn't manage to achieve, and they have allowed these to overshadow their overall progress.

When I reel off a list of all their positive actions I see their face change as they realize they haven't been quite as unproductive as they originally thought. As human beings we are so hard on ourselves and habitually focus more on our so-called failures than we do on our victories. If you find yourself being harsh, remind yourself of all your past successes; bring back the memory of the event, feel the feeling you felt at the time, let endorphins saturate your entire body until you feel powerful again.

HAND IT OVER

This is probably one of the most powerful things you can do when you feel rooted to the spot by fear. Remember, achieving your goals in the mind alone isn't the best route; you can undoubtedly create wonderful things in your mind, but when you add a little dose of spirit your journey becomes a much smoother ride. Spirit is your ultimate fulfilment; it knows what you need; it knows what you want and, most importantly, it knows exactly how to get you there. But when we allow our minds to rule our daily lives, spirit cannot present itself to us and we miss out on the miracle. You do not have to work out everything yourself.

You are not alone. There is a wonderful higher power lying dormant, right now, which you can call upon any time you need to. Why ignore this? It's like telling a pilot you want to fly the plane yourself when you're not a qualified pilot!

If you find yourself feeling fearful, concerned, worried, anxious, frustrated, let down, apathetic, disappointed, upset or whatever – hand over and wait for the feeling to pass. Why hold on to feelings that are not going to serve you? When you let go, the issues or problems will dissolve into nothingness, quickly enabling you to move on.

When I feel stuck or negative, rather than trying to 'fix' the problem myself I have learned to hand over and wait for fresh inspiration. I do this by simply meditating or quieting the mind using the techniques described in Chapter 6. As Einstein once said, 'You can never solve a problem on the level on which it was created.' Remember, your mind is programmed and is full of bad beliefs, concepts, thoughts, fears and perceptions which get in the way of you living the life you truly want. Yes, you can do affirmations, create evidence and the like, all these techniques undeniably work, but the more you can become aware of spirit, the more harmonious and pleasurable your journey will become and the quicker things will start to change. In short, spirit can rewire your brain for you, if you let it.

So stop trying to fix the issues or problems in your life, raise your awareness heavenwards and remember you are a spiritual being.

Life is actually incorporeal, not corporeal as we've all been led to believe. Once you recognize and start to experience this, your fears will dissolve forever.

WHERE IS ALL THE MONEY TO COME FROM?

We're nearly at the end of book, but there is one important element we haven't touched on – the dreaded issue of money! When we set out to make big life changes, money invariably comes into the equation at some time or another. Whether it's money to retrain, travel or buy a particular item, most of us will need some extra cash at some point. In fact, this is probably one of the greatest excuses that people use for not making changes to their lives. Most of us have mortgages, bills, loans, credit cards to pay, and naturally these things can feel very stifling and restricting. Unfortunately, modern living has allowed us to live way beyond our means, and of course this reduces our options in life because we become tied down by our own financial restraints. Just because you have this amazing, new, exciting goal to achieve doesn't mean you should run out and quit your job, or stop paying your bills. All these things still need to be maintained. As romantic as it may seem to just tell your boss to shove the job, or to sell up and move to Australia, it's not really wise to leap without thinking first as it will only add to your stress levels and put more pressure on you in the long run. There is nothing more depressing or demotivating than looking at a dwindling bank account when you're desperately trying to stay focused on achieving your goals. When you are constantly reminded of your lack of money, life can feel frightening, terrifying and impossible, and your goals will suffer as a result. Lack of money is undoubtedly one of the chief things that bring people's goals to a grinding halt.

As I mentioned earlier, I clearly remember the moment when I found out how much my training was going to cost me, and momentarily I thought that was the end of my dream. But what I realized was, 'OK, so I haven't got all the money I need right now, so what? I just need to start saving every penny I've got. It might take me a little longer, but I'll get there eventually.' And this is exactly what I did. I was totally focused. I cut back on non-essential spending such as luxuries I didn't really need, set up a 'training course money pot' account and started saving everything I could each month. Within six months I had managed to claw enough money together to start my training.

You need to put together a basic financial plan of action because you need to be able to finance your goals and support yourself throughout any changes you make.

Work out how much your new life is going to cost you. There is always a way around it and things are never as impossible as they first look. If you are going to need extra money to pursue your goals, then make sure you add 'finances' as one of your strategies or milestones in your overall plan of action.

Exercise

Answer the following questions:

- *How much money will each of your goals cost you to achieve?*

- *How do you plan to finance this?*

- *What can you do to raise the money?*

- *Who can help you?*

Take your most recent bank statement and go through every item systemically, marking each item listed with either a '1', '2' or '3'. Number 1 indicates essential items, such as your mortgage, insurance or gas bill; basically, these are things that must be paid. Number 2 indicates items that aren't essential but still need paying, such as your home phone, mobile phone, food, satellite TV bill and so on. Finally, number 3 indicates non-essential spending, such as meals out, new clothes, hair appointments, DVDs and the like.

Once you've made this analysis, first concentrate your efforts on items numbered '2' and '3' to see where reductions can be made. Perhaps you can change your hairdresser for someone cheaper, maybe you can change your mobile phone provider, perhaps instead of going out for dinner three times a month you can do this only once. Maybe now is the time to stop smoking or start taking sandwiches into work instead of buying them every day.

Once you've done this, take some time to address the items numbered '1' on your statement, such as your mortgage or gas bill, and see whether there are

any ways you can save money by changing supplier or provider. When you look hard enough you will be able to save towards your new venture. At the end of the day it all boils down to your overall commitment: 'How much do I really want change in my life?' 'How much do I really want to achieve my goals?'

Exercise

List ten ways in which you can start saving for your new life.

Most people who decide to make big life changes have to remain in their full-time jobs while they retrain at weekends or in the evenings, or make some other kind of sacrifice. But it's important to keep the money coming in to maintain your survival. It's only a temporary measure; it isn't forever. Be sensible and preserve your safety net. Eventually the day will come when you're finally ready to break free of your old life; you will be ready and bright-eyed to start your new one. So be patient.

WHAT ARE YOU WAITING FOR?

There is very little left to say, other than, 'What are you waiting for?' The time has come for you to make your dreams come true. It's over to you now: your life is in your own hands. It's time to start living with more vim and vigour than ever before. It's time to stop tip-toeing around the edges of life and jump in with both feet. From this day forward, commit yourself to taking more risks, saying 'Yes' to more opportunities and expanding your comfort zone far wider than ever before.

> *There is nothing holding you back now other than you!*

A Final Word

You're almost there!

So you've created your life-changing goals, and you're well on your way to making the necessary changes. Your mindset is starting to alter, and those around you are beginning to see the 'new you' emerge. There's no turning back now; you've done the hard bit and you feel fantastic.

Does your evolving journey ever end? I don't honestly know, as I'm still travelling. What I can tell you is, as you live your life in line with your blueprint, and ultimately your inner spirit, your life will be blessed in ways you simply cannot imagine. Things will fall into place, life will become a breeze and people will start asking, 'What's your secret?'

But, remember, we are human beings; we are here to experience duality and we are here to experience life at both ends of the spectrum: hot and cold, light and dark, happiness and sorrow, success and failure. We can't experience one without the other or life would be hideously dull. Life will sometimes throw us tough challenges, but how we deal with them is the key. The bills will still need paying, the dog will still need walking and the kids will still drive you mad. This is life. Appreciate it for what it is. See order and beauty in everything. And, when things get a little rough, let go and know that it will soon pass. What I've found is, when things go wrong, all your good work tends to go out of the window. As soon as you feel exposed or weak your Inner Critic will reappear from nowhere, cranking up its volume and absorbing every good thought in your head. Your old programming resurfaces and you start creating all sorts of odd behaviours and habits. When this happens it's time to stop and take time out.

I remember a few months into my newly self-employed life I went to a ladies' networking event at my local shopping centre. At the time I was frantically attending every networking or social event I could to try and attract new clients. As I sat in a circle of noisy women all trying to get their story heard, I suddenly felt very vulnerable and alien to my new surroundings. I heard my Inner Critic pipe up and say, 'What on Earth are you doing here, Louise? Stop pretending and get back to your proper job!' I had spent years tucked away in a nice cosy office without the need to step out of my comfort zone, and there I was trying to encourage people I didn't know that they needed my services. I spent most of the morning in a world of my own, waiting for the meeting to end. I just wanted to run and hide. I wanted to go home. I wanted my old, comfortable, familiar life back.

In hindsight, it was just one of those days where I allowed my inner fears to take hold of me. And this will inevitably happen for you at some point. There have been numerous occasions when my goals felt colossal and far from reach, but this is normal for everyone who is committed to making big life changes. There will be times when we just want to recoil and retreat back to our old life where everything is cosy and secure – where we know where we stand. But slowly but surely, as we keep ploughing on, it gets easier and easier until the discomfort of the early days is just a distant memory. I promise it will all be worth it in the end when you look back in astonishment at the remarkable journey you have undertaken. Just keep your vision firmly locked on where it is you're going and you cannot go wrong!

No one has ever said living the life of your dreams is easy. It takes drive and determination, persistence and patience, faith and trust in the wonderful power within us, but, most importantly, it takes action. The greatest risk, however, comes from doing nothing at all. Life is for living, not enduring!

The time has come for us to part and for you finally to let go of my hand. It's been wonderful travelling with you this far, but you are now holding everything you need to create the life you want, the life you know you deserve. When you feel a little wobbly, as we all do from time to time, remember I'm always here. Just pick up this book and keep reading until you feel strong again.

My only advice is, keep this book with you, stay focused, remain aware, connect to your inner spirit, go with the flow and, most importantly, enjoy the ride.

See you on the other side. You are your own fairy godmother, don't ever forget that!

Louise x

Resources

CONTACT LOUISE PRESLEY-TURNER

For further details on workshops, talks, weekend retreats, corporate, business or one-to-one coaching, visit www.thegameoflife.co.uk or call 01746 71 61 51.

To join the mailing list log on to www.thegameoflife.co.uk.

For a 90-minute one-to-one Discovery Coaching Session email louise@thegameoflife.co.uk.

FURTHER READING

General

Carol Adrienne, *The Purpose of Your Life* (Thorsons)

Lynn Grabhorn, *Excuse Me, Your Life Is Waiting: The Power of Positive Feelings* (Mobius)

Suzy Greaves, *The Big Peace* (Hay House)

Louise L. Hay, *The Power Is Within You* (Hay House); *Heal Your Body* (Hay House)

Susan Jeffers, *Feel the Fear and Do It Anyway* (Vermilion)

Byron Katie and Stephen Mitchell, *Loving What Is: How Four Questions Can Change Your Life* (Rider)

Paul McKenna, *Change Your Life in 7 Days* (Bantam Press); *Instant Confidence* (Bantam Press)

Allison Mitchell, *Time Management for Manic Mums* (Hay House)

Professor Karen J. Pine and Simonne Gnessen, *Sheconomics* (Headline)

Eckhart Tolle, *A New Earth* (Penguin)
John Williams, *Screw Work, Let's Play* (Prentice Hall Business)
Marianne Williamson, *The Gift of Change* (Element)

Business

Duncan Bannatyne, *Anyone Can Do It: My Story* (Orion)
Jack Canfield with Janet Switzer, *The Success Principles: How to Get from Where You Are to Where You Want to Be* (Element)
Peter Jones, *Tycoon* (Hodder)
Paul McKenna, *I Can Make You Rich* (Bantam Press)
Cheryl D. Rickman and Dame Anita Roddick, *The Small Business Start-up Workbook: A Step-by-step Guide to Starting the Business You've Dreamed of* (How To Books)

The Spiritual Quest

Rhonda Byrne, *The Secret* (Simon & Schuster)
Dr Wayne W. Dyer, *Change Your Thoughts, Change Your Life* (Hay House)
Masaru Emoto, *The Hidden Messages in Water* (Pocket Books)
Barbel Mohr, *The Cosmic Ordering Service* (Mobius)
John Parkin, *F**k It: The Ultimate Spiritual Way* (Hay House)
Candace B. Pert, *Molecules of Emotion: Why You Feel the Way You Feel* (Pocket Books)
Paul Roland, *How to Meditate* (Hamlyn)
Sharon Salzberg, *The Power of Meditation* (Hay House)
Doreen Virtue, *Chakra Clearing: Awakening Your Spiritual Power to Know and Heal*: Book + CD (Hay House); *Healing with the Angels: How the Angels Can Assist You in Every Area of Your Life* (Hay House)
Neale Donald Walsch, *Conversations with God*, Books 1, 2 and 3 (Mobius)

DVDS

The Celestine Prophecy
Conversations with God
Deepak Chopra – The Seven Spiritual Laws of Success
The Secret
The Shift
What the Bleep Do We Know!?
You Can Heal Your Life

ABOUT THE AUTHOR

Louise Presley-Turner is a leading life coach whose unique approach helps people who are ready for real change to transform their lives. Featured in the UK's top media, her unique style of coaching has produced some amazing results, helping clients to define their goals and create new ways of living, with amazing success.

Not only do her coaching programmes provide a fantastic kick-start, but they also take you on an exciting and revealing inner journey. They really help you to get to know yourself better, empowering you to navigate your life in the right direction and produce positive results, quickly.

Louise is married with two beautiful children. She has a great love for learning new things, reading books and spirituality. She lives each day to the full, with a smile on her face, knowing that she is being true to herself and following her passion in life.

Get your free life coaching exercises today by joining the Game of Life Club at www.thegameoflife.co.uk